T0339824

NEUTRAL GROUND

Neutral Ground

A Political History
of
Espionage Fiction

Brett F. Woods

Algora Publishing
New York

© 2008 by Algora Publishing.
All Rights Reserved
www.algora.com

No portion of this book (beyond what is permitted by
Sections 107 or 108 of the United States Copyright Act of 1976)
may be reproduced by any process, stored in a retrieval system,
or transmitted in any form, or by any means, without the
express written permission of the publisher.

ISBN-13: 978-0-87586-533-1 (trade paper)
ISBN-13: 978-0-87586-534-8 (hard cover)
ISBN-13: 978-0-87586-535-5 (ebook)

Library of Congress Cataloging-in-Publication Data —

Woods, Brett F.
    Neutral ground : a political history of espionage fiction / by Brett F.
Woods.
        p. cm.
    Includes bibliographical references and index.
    ISBN 978-0-87586-533-1 (trade paper: alk. paper) — ISBN 978-0-87586-
534-8 (hard cover: alk. paper) — ISBN 978-0-87586-535-5 (ebook) 1. Spy stories,
English—History and criticism. 2. Spy stories, American—History and criticism.
3. Politics and literature—Great Britain—History—20th century. 4. Politics
and literature—United States—History—20th century. 5. World politics in
literature. 6. Espionage in literature. 7. Spies in literature. I. Title.

    PR830.S65W66 2007
    823'.087209—dc22

                        2007018848

Front Cover: Man Wearing Trench Coat, Hat, and Sunglasses Standing
Under Surveillance Camera
Image: © Sebastian Pfuetze/zefa/Corbis

Printed in the United States

ACKNOWLEDGEMENTS

I began this monograph while studying in England and I am indebted to numerous individuals associated with the Department of Literature at the University of Essex: Professor Richard Gray; Drs. Leon Burnett and Jacqueline Kaye; Roger Howard, playwright, critic, and founder of the Essex writer's residency program; and Norman Schwenk, former convenor of creative writing at the University of Wales, Cardiff. Individually and collectively their suggestions, critiques, and endorsements were central to the completion of my various projects.

Also at Essex, Dr. Adrian May and Elizabeth Weall: Elizabeth for her friendship, her candid observations on my research, and for leading me through the administrative maze and particular personality that besets British academia; and Adrian, a contemporary, for his encouragement, wit, and humor. To paraphrase one of Adrian's anecdotes, "You're an author, so go auth!" And this, I suppose, is what historical research and writing is really all about.

A special note of appreciation to Dr. Joseph Allard, my principal advisor at Essex. The pubs of Wivenhoe aside, his criticisms and considerations, but most of all his approach to the study of literature — that it is indeed central to understanding the various historical milieus — kept things in perspective.

Finally, to Helen, Maren, and Connor, for their collective support and for the numerous indulgences that made possible my pursuit of "things British."

Brett F. Woods
Santa Fe, New Mexico

Espionage is the world's second oldest profession and just as honorable as the first.

— Michael J. Barrett, *Journal of Defence and Diplomacy*, February 1984

TABLE OF CONTENTS

xi

Introduction

Since its popular recognition in the early twentieth century, the spy novel has served as a vehicle to pursue the darker political imaginations of the Western world. Drawn from reality, revealing what is generally veiled, it seeks to provide a brief glimpse into society's political underbelly through the application of international intrigues, questionable alliances, and, on not few occasions, spirited doses of sex, violence and, of course, murder. It is an arena where the moods are gray, the settings circumscribed and the heroes — if indeed there are heroes — emerge as ordinary individuals who are not much different than the people they oppose: common men following dangerous paths through uncertain times.[1] As John Le Carré's fictional Leamas cynically remarks of the players: "A squalid procession of vain fools, traitors too, yes...people who play cowboys and Indians to brighten their rotten little lives."[2]

This commentary is titled *Neutral Ground: A Political History of Espionage Fiction* and, accordingly, it offers a brief examination of the evolution of the espionage story. In particular, it explores how, beginning with the 1821 publication of James Fenimore Cooper's *The Spy: A Tale of Neutral Ground*, and continuing to John Le Carré in the present day,

---

1 Walker 2006.
2 Le Carré 1965, 229.

extrapolations of certain real world political events — the American Revolution, British Imperialism, the World Wars, and the Cold War, for example — have consistently and significantly threaded their way through the fabric of the genre.

The authors discussed share a similar approach to their stories in that they, either overtly or implicitly, base fundamental story requisites such as plot, theme, and conspiratorial contexts upon some measure of factual geopolitical occurrence, thus creating hybrid texts that blend fictional premise with certain nonfiction elements. When cast astride what has become known as the "conspiratorial approach to history," this subtle blending of fact and fiction emerges as a medium in which documents, dates, operational procedure, technology, and other representations of reality seamlessly coexist with invented characters and events. And though valid historical accounts select, arrange and make value judgments on information, the spy novelist, with an eye to structure, pacing and character development, bends the documentary record and constructs carefully crafted narratives that, to all intents and purposes, assume complete historical authority.

In the most general sense, the evolution of the spy novel emerges in the guise of a continuum and, taken together, the body of work constitutes one of the most popular forms of entertainment in literature. Consequently, the selection of authors in this commentary involves some criteria. I have elected to include only those authors who generally are credited with making significant contributions to the genre's progression. This, of course, is not to say that there are not dozens, if not hundreds, of other espionage novelists who have — or have not — contributed to the genre's evolution. But due to the proliferation of the genre since the turn of the twentieth century, a sheer analytic approach seems impractical and will doubtless lead to misinterpretation.

Accordingly, I have attempted to trace the genre chronologically and to proceed by a series of associations, links, and causes and effects, which, taken together, will illustrate the genre's continuing dependence upon world geopolitical alignments and relevant historical constructs. Chapter 1 will provide a brief overview of the genre's historical foundations; Chapter 2, the emergence of espionage fiction as a legitimate literary genre; Chapter 3, the genre against the backdrop of World War I;

Chapter 4, the maturing of the genre; Chapter 5, post-World War II conspiracy theory; Chapter 6, the Cold War era; and, finally, Chapter 7 explores the more popular variations on the genre's themes.

As the selected texts will hopefully illustrate, the traditional distinctions between fact and fiction, if selectively and subtly addressed, can become little more than matters of perspective. Moreover, they also serve to highlight the hybrid — fact *and* fiction — nature of the contemporary spy novel, particularly with respect to the influences of war, politics, and international affairs on the evolution of the genre.

Of course, as in the case of any subjective exercise, errors in fact, transcription, and interpretation, remain entirely my responsibility.

Chapter 1. The Roots of Espionage Fiction

> With the world in its present condition of extreme unrest
> and changing friendships and antagonisms, and with our greatly
> reduced and weak military forces, it is more than ever vital to us
> to have good and timely information.
> — Winston Churchill, letter to Lloyd George, 19 March 1920

Graham Greene, one of the recognized masters of the spy novel,
dedicated his classic anthology, *The Spy's Bedside Book*, to "the immortal memory of William Le Queux and John Buchan."[3] Maybe, but
some fifty years later, the fame of both Buchan and Le Queux seems
debatable. Nonetheless, Greene was commending two pioneers of the
genre and also reminding us of that time in history when espionage
fiction first began to emerge as a distinct literary genre, for it was during the Le Queux-Buchan years, amid the turbulent drama of the first
decades of the twentieth century, that world geopolitical events first
achieved some measure of acceptance as viable and relevant scenarios
from which to glean the rich stock of motifs, plots and character types
that now distinguish the contemporary spy novel.[4] So while Le Queux
and Buchan may well be forgotten, they were major influences in the
evolution of the spy novel and, as followed by the likes Joseph Conrad,

---

3 Greene 1957, ii.
4 Wark 1998, 1199.

Somerset Maugham and even Greene himself, their contributions to the genre were undeniably significant.[5]

GENESIS ~

Over two thousand years ago, Sun Tzu suggested that, "Knowledge of the enemy's dispositions can only be obtained from other men."[6] And while a seemingly simple observation, even today it remains a fundamental principle of espionage tradecraft. The word *spy*, for which there is a single character in the Chinese language, had as its original meaning in ancient China that of "a chink," "a crack" or "crevice."[7] From any of these meanings one can derive the sense of a peephole, so it would seem that the earliest Chinese conception of a spy is, very simply, one who peeps through a crack. For this reason, it is perhaps appropriate to look to ancient China as background to espionage fiction because it is here, as far back as 450 BC, that the earliest textbook, not only on the arts of war but also espionage and the organization of a "secret service," was written. This was the *Ping Fa* of Sun Tzu (personal name Sun Wu), a military strategist and general who lived in China sometime during the Warring States period (c. 453–221 BC).[8] Considered the oldest military treatise in history, the dissertation contemplates the close relationship between political considerations and military policy. Not only is it a valuable guide to the arts of espionage down through the ages in China, but continues to be required reading for contemporary students, and practitioners, of espionage.

Admittedly, the phrase *one who peeps through a crack* is somewhat of a one-dimensional definition of espionage; nonetheless, this is precisely what the author of the spy novel must be able to do, for at its best, this genre of literature is indeed a peepshow — a brief glimpse into the dark underside of political discourse. But, too, it is a glimpse that changes

---

5 There exists a unique, mutually beneficial relationship between the espionage agency and the spy novelist. Espionage agencies profit because the novelist generally legitimizes the spy's activities, thus contributing to the public perception that, in an imperfect world, the spy's activities, however distasteful, are necessary. For the novelist the benefit is even more straightforward: espionage stories are financially profitable.

6 From *The Art of War*.

7 McCormick 1977, 1.

8 The *Ping Fa* is better known by the title *The Art of War*.

its perception from age to age, from generation to generation, and from place to place.[9]

Spies and saboteurs have existed for thousands of years and their surreptitious activities have been conducted at the behest of church, state, business, and for any number of other lesser factions. Certainly these people were well known in ancient Israel for the Old Testament reveals that both Joshua and Moses employed teams of spies. A little further north and a bit later in time, Alexander the Great and Julius Caesar both rather handsomely profited from their espionage apparatuses. This trend continues up through Daniel Defoe, who more or less started British intelligence in the early 1700s; to Rose Greenhow who spied the American Union Army into disaster at Bull Run; to Mata Hari of World War I fame; to Allen Dulles and Dusko Popov, the World War II spymasters; and eventually through the era of the Soviet-sponsored, Burgess-Blunt-Maclean-Philby "Cambridge Spy Ring" that penetrated British Intelligence during the Cold War era.

Even more recently, we have witnessed the detection of several Soviet spies who have penetrated various American intelligence agencies: Central Intelligence Agency (CIA) employees Edward Howard and Aldrich Ames, John Walker of the US Navy and Robert Hanssen of the Federal Bureau of Investigation, among numerous others. Yet those mentioned here are but a notable few, for there have been untold thousands of spies operating at one time or the other — or in one place or the other — over the last several millennia and, to be sure, the fruits of their labors were well received by their employers.

Historically, the routine of espionage is generally directed to obtaining something (information) or neutralizing something (people or property) in the homeland or conquered territory of a particular enemy. But it is also a culture of sorts wherein the end not only justifies the means, but also serves as a kind of furtive absolution wherein the proscribing character of espionage — at least in the eyes of the spy and his own country — is marginalized due to its ostensible importance to national survival. This mindset was particularly well put in a 1775 letter of Nathan Hale who observed: "Every kind of service necessary

---

9 Ibid.

to the public good becomes honorable by being necessary."[10] As for the kind of people who become spies, the words of Sun Tzu are as valid today as they were 2500 years ago: "As living spies, we must recruit men who are intelligent, but appear to be stupid; who seem to be dull, but are strong in heart; men who are agile, vigorous, hardy, and brave; well-versed in lowly matters and able to endure hunger, cold, filth, and humiliation."[11]

Motives for being a secret agent have ranged from money, to vengeance for particular wrongs, to the idea of making mankind safe for a particular ideology. Public glory has not necessarily been an incentive primarily because of the clandestine aspect of the business. Too, the life of a spy can be a very lonely and dull affair, with most operatives relegated to becoming little more than cogs in bureaucratic machines run from afar with the principal necessities being order and routine — an uninspiring reality that leaves little room for James Bonds in everyday clandestine operations. And while this is not to imply that the James Bond-types of operatives have never existed, it is suggested that their numbers have been substantially fewer than readers of espionage fiction might be led to expect.

Yet despite the historical presence of secret agents, the fictional literature of their exploits — real and imagined — has been primarily a twentieth century phenomenon. This is largely due to the fact that prior to the twentieth century the spy story was, if not derided, at least ignored. Why? It seems that there were certain moral and societal factors at play: espionage was regarded as one of the more distasteful social enterprises and, therefore, no spy should rightly be considered as a hero. Nor was it even considered desirable that the chief villain of a story should be a spy. A thief, yes; a murderer, most certainly; but a spy was the nineteenth-century equivalent of the sexual pervert and the most ostracized character in literature.[12]

Western democracies, with their presumptions of openness, have never been comfortable with the unavoidable secrecy of intelligence

---

10 Nathan Hale, a soldier of the American Revolution, was hanged, by order of British General William Howe, as a spy, in the city of New York, on September 22, 1776.

11 Tzu 1910.

12 McCormick and Fletcher 1990, 3.

and espionage. Moreover, the intelligence community is not without its detractors, both for what it is and for what it is not. Historically, espionage activities are dangerous and prone to scandal, illegality, or both.[13] As a result, espionage remained, at least until the late nineteenth century, a political nether region, and an unsavory arena in which to develop fictional heroes. Spies, then, be they heroes *or* villains, were considered well outside the political constraints of civilized society. So while, at least publicly, most ascribed to the oft-quoted Stimson observation that "gentlemen do not read other gentlemen's mail," it is this same secrecy, danger, scandal and illegality that provided ample raw material for early espionage fiction.[14]

The spy novel, though it seemingly burst forth with great sudden-ness in the early 1900s, has in fact two primary antecedents: (1) the anarchist and terrorist fiction of the late nineteenth century; and (2) Victorian pornography, with its locked rooms, secret amorality, and the general suggestion of threat to established values. And even earlier than these, there was one explicit experiment with the espionage genre: *The Spy: A Tale of the Neutral Ground* (1821), by the American writer James Fenimore Cooper.[15] Although *The Spy* failed to generate any immediate literary succession, it is arguably the first espionage novel and with it, we witness the genre's initial engagement with geopolitical reality: the backdrop of the American Revolution in New York State.[16]

But while the genre of spy fiction was slow to materialize, in 1894 the reality of the existence of espionage was brought to the forefront by the monumental scandal in France known as "The Dreyfus Affair," which revealed German espionage activities in France.[17] Once the idea

---

13 Britain's Philby and Profumo spy scandals of the 1950s and early 1960s are repre-sentative examples.

14 Henry L. Stimson was the United States Secretary of War during World War II. (Isaacson and Thomas 1986, 182)

15 Wark 1998, 1199.

16 Cooper's *The Spy* is further discussed in Chapter 2.

17 The Dreyfus Affair was a stinging humiliation that reshaped French politics in the 1890s and early 1900s. In 1894, the French army accused one of its officers, Captain Alfred Dreyfus, of selling military secrets to Germany. A court-martial condemned Dreyfus to life imprisonment on Devil's Island in French Guyana. It was subsequently proven that Dreyfus had been framed and the French novel-ist Emile Zola stunned Paris by publishing an article that condemned France's military leadership for framing Dreyfus, who was eventually released from imprisonment.

of secret operatives was thus established in the public domain, British writers, with an eye to the Crown's perceived geopolitical vulnerability, began to turn their attention to espionage scenarios. In the early 1900s, when the espionage novel eventually did emerge, it did so from a firmly British base, and British writers were to hold a near monopoly on the genre for many decades. This was a tribute to the power of the London publishing industry, to Britain's status as a world power, and, just as important, to the popular fears that attached themselves to a nation beginning to suffer from imperial overstretch. The contours of this new literary genre were first suggested by two key works, Rudyard Kipling's *Kim* (1901), and Erskine Childers' *The Riddle of the Sands* (1903). Both novels wedded tales of adventure to visions of Britain's political standing, mediated by the figure of the spy.[18]

Definitions ~

One of the difficulties in detailing the evolution of the spy novel is that it is no simple thing to pinpoint the beginning of the genre or, for that matter, to precisely define what is and what is not to be classified as essential to the development of the genre. In truth, the definition of *espionage fiction* is somewhat more elusive than that of detective fiction which can generally be identified in precise terms, and has therefore come to be accepted as a branch of literature. But not so the espionage story which, in some circles, has been treated with little more than derision. And although some of the practitioners of espionage fiction are themselves authors of great distinction in the broader world of literature — Joseph Conrad, G.K. Chesterton, and Somerset Maugham, among them — it is reasonably assured that not one of their espionage characters is likely to achieve the institutional stature of Arthur Conan Doyle's fictional detective Sherlock Holmes. Why? This seems to stem from the fact that the "espionage story" — when contrasted with the detective story — is in itself somewhat of a misnomer.

A detective story is built entirely around the character of the detective. Without him, there would be no story. And he can survive indefinitely. But the main figure in a spy story, if he *is* technically a spy,

---

18 Wark 1998, 1199.

cannot be expected to have a lengthy operational life: sooner or later, he (or she) will eventually be discovered. But, more to the point, the main figure might not be a spy at all: he may be a counter-espionage agent like James Bond, or an intelligence chief sitting at a desk in London, Washington or Moscow, controlling a network of spies, but not doing any spying himself. In fact, when we speak of the spy novel, we may be well talking of spy-catchers as well as spies; of double and triple agents as well as agents; and, at least peripherally, of hired killers, planters of misinformation, and sometimes even of that unassuming little fellow at the corner antique book shop who operates a kind of letter-box or dead drop for agents.[19]

Espionage novels, by contemporary standards, are generally considered to be "thrillers" and, at least on face, are similar to certain police procedurals and more mainstream political novels: they center on some nefarious activity and build tension though the combination of suspense and intrigue, coupled with action and excitement.[20] There is the presumption — again, real or imagined — of a threat to someone, some place, or some thing, and the conflict is created through aggressive engagement. This is comparable to the scenario expressed in Frederick Forsyth's *The Day of the Jackal* (1971) in which the plot structure parallels two central characters who are sketched as binary opposites. As the jackal goes through different disguises and assembles his rifle for the assassination of French President Charles de Gaulle, the policeman is assembling evidence of these activities and closing the pursuit.[21]

Critics find the spy story remarkably straightforward in its structure and appeal, and the fit between the standard pattern of the folktale and the modern spy novel is a strikingly precise one.[22] To achieve the requisite "structural simplicity" criteria of the spy novel, authors, to greater or lesser degrees, generally follow a set formula: introduce the hero, provide difficulties, and resolve impediments.[23] People read spy novels because reading them releases tension. Each novel has a beginning and an end — unlike much of everyday life that tends to meander

---

19 McCormick and Fletcher 1990, 3.
20 Benvenuti and Rizzoni 1982, 57.
21 Landrum 1999, 27.
22 Merry 1997, 235.
23 Winks 1986, vi.

on — and evils and perils are set right through commitment and competence, aided by virtue and luck. To this end, five general elements in espionage fiction can be identified:[24]

1. It must include poetic justice and there must be a simple yet shocking view of the world and events.
2. It must include banality and some measure of humor.
3. Both the plausible and implausible are present, with the implausible perhaps a vehicle to facilitate the success of the hero.
4. It allows the reader to enter a "primary world" and does not need a superfluity of facts or outsize villains. The primary world is made up of a love of adventure, a patriotic struggle against evil, the opportunity for individual heroism, and the prospect for reward by love.
5. The novel pits gentlemen against professionals, noting that after World War II the hero also generally becomes a trained professional. The hero's own peril is always central, and the hero is vulnerable and can be hurt.[24]

Of course, not all novels contain every element. Still, as a basic framework, these observations appear to have merit, particularly in the study of some of the genre's earlier authors such as Childers, Oppenheim, Le Queux and Buchan wherein the hero — in an ideological and patriotic sense — emerges as a vehicle for competitive individuality which is drawn from, as well as justified by, a tangible fear of conspiracy.[25] Yet, through the hero, this same ideology and patriotism represses the fear and offers a solution to offset the conspiracy, thus preventing the disruption of society.

The specificity of the spy novel grounds it in an ideology designed to compensate for conspiracy. It is not to give false answers to real problems, but to pose problems in such a way that the recommendations one wished to make in the first place appear to correspond to a real problem.[26] This relationship between ideology and conspiracy is typified by Erskine Childers' *Riddle of the Sands* (1903). The author, concerned with German militarism, sought to direct the British Admiral-

---

24 Harper 1969, 9.
25 In the novels of Childers, Oppenheim, Le Queux, and Buchan the "conspiracy" is repeatedly represented by the threat of a German invasion of England or, minimally, German espionage activities directed against the British Crown.
26 Palmer 1979, 204.

ty's attention to its own lack of intelligence information on German in-tentions and capabilities. To do so, Childers crafted a fictional scenario in which individuals on a yacht trip observe suspicious German naval activity off the coast of the Frisian Islands. Upon publication, the novel was so successful as to prompt an internal Admiralty review of its own capabilities, and to sanction a survey of the Frisian area which resulted in the implementation of enhanced naval intelligence activities. With the novel, Childers proposed no false solutions to real problems, but satisfied his intentions — drawing the Admiralty's attention German naval activities — by, in the fictional context, recommending a survey of the Frisian Islands, which the Admiralty ultimately conducted.[27]

As the genre evolved, and in the attempt to construct some measure of uniqueness in scenario, espionage authors presented any number of plot variations with "the conspiracy" being limited not solely to con-ventional espionage, but spilling over to any number of political sce-narios such as *coups d'état* and assassination threats to Heads of State. The variants possible in this form are numberless and, by either change or design, have predictably led to some measure of ambiguity between politics and criminal activity. But, regardless of plot manipulations, in its purest form — and particularly in the British sense — the spy novel remains grounded in the culture of imperialism, in the anxiety of foreign invasion, and in the refinement of surveillance on the domes-tic population and external enemies. And here, it seems, is perhaps the most functional place to begin the genre's history.

---

27 Childers' *The Riddle of the Sands* is further discussed in Chapter Three.

Chapter 2. Evolution of the Genre

> Fact is a poor storyteller. It starts a story at haphazard, gen-
> erally long before the beginning, rambles on inconsequently and
> tails off leaving loose ends hanging about, without a conclusion.
> — W. Somerset Maugham, Preface to *Ashenden or The British
> Agent*, c. 1951

Taken as a body of literature, the spy story emerges as a particularly obvious juncture where the codes of ideology and fiction run together. It provides a forum for a politics that dare not, in every case, speak its name: a public voice for furtive histories, and an apologetic or damn-ing script for nationalism and imperialism and clandestine meddling in international affairs.[28] When viewed from this perspective, the rela-tionships between the spy novel, world political events and the engage-ment of reality-based fictional scenarios — be they drawn against the backdrop of James Fenimore Cooper's eighteenth century New York or John Le Carré's twentieth century Berlin — emerge as fundamental elements in evolution of the genre.

At first glance, there is a case, albeit marginal, for considering Lo Kuan-chung of the Yuan dynasty (1260-1341) as the first author of a spy story. His text, the *San Kuo Yen-I* — translated as *The Romance of the Three Kingdoms* (1991) — is a lengthy historical novel, its plot being based on

---

28 McTiernan 1997.

events covering the period from AD 168-265. It opens with the threatened decline of the Han dynasty in the reign of Ling Ti and the insurrection of the Yellow Turbans. The story details how, in the period, directors of spies consulted the *I Ching*, and its pages are filled with ingenious spy plots, espionage techniques and double agents.[29]

San Kuo contains many examples of the kind of deadlock that often ensued as a result of warring between espionage groups of equal astuteness. "I would rather betray the whole world than let the world betray me," declares Ts'ao Chen, the villain-hero of *San Kuo*.[30] Ts'ao then proceeds to kill the entire family of his host because he believes — quite misguidedly, as it turns out — that they are plotting against him. But while there are indeed numerous references to espionage in the text, the *San Kuo* is not, in the strictest sense, an espionage novel. On the contrary, it is as much a classical, philosophical treatise and a work of history as it is a tale about spies. Further, and probably more relevant to this discussion, its accounts of espionage ruses are, in all probability, more factual than fictional.[31] Accordingly, it is not until the 1821 publication of James Fenimore Cooper's *The Spy* that we find the first true example of the espionage novel.

JAMES FENIMORE COOPER ~

> The escape of the English spy has been reported to me, but his arrest is unimportant, compared with the duty I now assign you.
> — James Fenimore Cooper, *The Spy*, c. 1821

James Fenimore Cooper (1789-1851) was America's first successful popular novelist. The son of the prominent federalist William Cooper, founder of the Cooperstown settlement, Cooper was educated at Yale in preparation for a genteel life as a federalist gentleman. However, after his father's untimely death in an 1809 duel, Cooper quickly squandered his inheritance and, at age thirty, was on the verge of bankruptcy. He decided to try his hand at writing as a career, carefully modeling his work after Sir Walter Scott's successful Waverley novels. Cooper's first

---

29 McCormick 1977, 2.
30 Kuan-chung 1977, 2.
31 McCormick 1977, 2.

novel, *Precaution* (1820), a domestic comedy set in England, lost money;
but Cooper had discovered his vocation and for his second book he
chose a subject closer to home: *The Spy: A Tale of Neutral Ground* (1821), a
novel about the American Revolution (1775–1783) in New York State.[32]
The Spy was successful both in the United States and abroad.

As the first novelist to explore the theme of espionage, Cooper had
no examples and instead relied on the conventions of other genres —
primarily the historical adventure — to explore the duplicity and clandestine nature of espionage. And it is this juxtaposition of historical
adventure with Cooper's own moral, political, and social ratification
of spying that provides a seminal example of the seesaw relationship
between literary form and applied ideology: each exerts its own force,
but neither escapes the pull of the other.[33]

Inspired by the accusations of corruption leveled against the men
who captured British Major John André, Cooper's novel centers on
Harry Birch, a common man wrongly suspected by well-born patriots
of being a spy for the British.[34] Even George Washington, who supports
Birch, misreads the man, and when Washington offers him payment
for information vital to colonial interests, Birch scorns the money and
asserts that his actions are motivated not by financial reward but by
his dedication to the fight for independence. And it is in this passage
where Cooper proposes the novel's central theme: that a nation's sur-

---

32 Yela, 2001.

33 McTiernan 1997.

34 Two of the more controversial spies in what are essentially romanticized tales
of the American Revolution would certainly be Benedict Arnold and Major
John André. In September 1780, on his return from West Point where he has
just schemed with Benedict Arnold to betray the American post at West Point,
Major John André is captured by American militiamen and brought to trial as a
spy. For the popular British officer, by now aide-de-camp to Sir Henry Clinton
— the British Commander in Chief — the arrest and charge must have come as
a rude shock; for he seems not to have understood, until late in the proceedings,
the seriousness of his situation. For Washington, angry at Arnold's treason,
mindful of the hanging of Nathan Hale, and needing to make clear to the British
the seriousness of rebel resolve, there is no ambiguity. During his detainment,
André claims to have been dressed as he is, a British officer; but at the trial, he is
formally charged with wearing the clothes of deceit: "That he changed his dress
within our lines, and under a feigned name, and in a disguised habit..." Such a
charge in wartime could bring only one punishment: death by hanging. André's
subsequent execution, at which the accused spy cut a noble, even tragic, figure
in the eyes of observers, drew outraged cries from all fronts, including some patriots (Richards 1991, 260-261).

vival, like its revolution, depends on judging people by their actions, not their class or reputations.

While *The Spy* may owe its particulars to story lines drawn from America's fledgling history, its narrative shape is most certainly reflective of the "neutral ground" described by Scottish novelist Sir Walter Scott (1771-1832), with Scott's highland's scenarios transplanted to landscapes of New York State. Like Scott, Cooper's story places its characters in a time and place of historical challenge. Instead of the 1745 Jacobite rebellion of Scott's *Waverley* (1814), we have the American Revolution, cast by Cooper as itself a kind of uprising. Both books particularize the great events of history in the lives of their major characters by motivating them to political action in response to the reality of their particular private experiences.[35]

As suggested by the title, the novel remains centered within that most ambiguous domain defined as the "neutral ground" — Cooper's term, adapted from Scott, for the region between opposing armies, controlled by neither but marked by their fluctuating power. Critics have generally read this phrase as a metaphor for the thematic conflicts and ambiguities that flourish in the absence of clear-cut authority and the various analyses have spawned all manner of spirited and lofty academic debate. Some, for instance, consider the *neutral ground* a "lawless moral landscape" that allows Cooper to present a pattern of moral contrasts.[36] Others venture a bit further, defining it as a "moral wasteland" where "conflicting principles are at war and the only law is might," a geographical space that "reflects the ambiguities" that "pervade the entire novel."[37]

---

35 Beginning with the publication of *The Spy*, reviewers began to term Cooper "the American Scott," a title which Cooper maintained "gives me more disgust than any other." Although largely unsuccessful, time and again, Cooper struggled to distance his writing from the Waverley novels. He distinguished, for example, his work from Scott's as the divergent productions of a republican and an aristocrat, cited Scott's unwillingness to engage American material, and characterized his own rather harshly reviewed novel, *The Heidenmauer* (1832), as better than two-thirds of the Waverley novels. In a review of Lockhart's posthumous edition of Scott's *Memoir* (1837), Cooper codified his rejection of Scott's literary paternity, and defended the extent of his attack by arguing that Scott's reactionary views disqualified him as a suitable writer for American and indeed for nineteenth-century audiences. Scott's reputation must, Cooper opined, be subjected to rigorous scrutiny and reappraisal (Kelly 1983, 38-39).

36 Dekker 1967, 34.

37 Ringe 1988, 12.

Other critics disagree, preferring to define the conflict somewhat differently: as a struggle between "individual integrity and social coherence" and the "social, historical, or psychological authority" embedded in the law.[38] Finally, still others consider the neutral ground to be a "lethal" environment where authority has broken down altogether, generating a "state of mind" in which all loyalties appear potentially treacherous.[39] In reality, probably all of these definitions, interpretations and postulations — however scholarly — are to some extent correct, with the concept of "neutral ground" emerging as some type of geographical or intellectual nether region that affords either opposing party the right of passage at their pleasure.[40] But, this said, while neutral ground may have been an accommodating venue in which to set a historical espionage adventure, Cooper still faced serious obstacles making the ever loathsome spy — even one with the best of patriotic intentions — a primary hero.

The role of Harvey Birch, *The Spy's* title character, perhaps best illustrates the conflicts and incongruities between Cooper's new American ideology and the times in which he wrote *The Spy*. To offset the early nineteenth century perception of "spies" as ignoble, inglorious creatures, Cooper attempts to portray Harvey Birch as an icon of American patriotism appropriate to historical adventure. To accomplish this, one of his strategies is to have morally unassailable characters compare Birch favorably to soldiers. Thus the noble rebel trooper from Virginia, Captain Lawton, praises Birch: "He [Birch] may be a spy — he must be one...but he has a heart above enmity, and a soul that would honor a gallant soldier."[41] This passage likens spies to soldiers. When a soldier breaks moral laws by killing, he is absolved by his country, and Cooper seeks to place Harvey Birch in precisely this same category. In another passage, Sergeant Hollister, one of Captain Lawton's men and an assiduous Christian, further pursues the soldier's — and, according to Cooper, the spy's — general amnesty: "As to killing a man in lawful battle,

---

38 Adams 1990, 40.

39 Rosenberg 1994, 136.

40 The hypothesis of "neutral ground" remains a fundamental concept in the spy story, and perhaps it is most easily illustrated by the city of Berlin as depicted in the various Cold War espionage stories.

41 Cooper 1997, 233.

why that is no more than doing one's duty. If the cause is wrong, the sin of such a deed, you know, falls on the nation..."[42] Cooper's message is straightforward. Insofar as a spy resembles a soldier, responsibility for his transgressions can be shifted onto the country and excused by their nationalistic ends.[43]

Cooper also burnishes Birch's character by portraying him as an honest, hard-working laborer, then a symbol of American strength and patriotism.[44] In a discussion with Sergeant Hollister about the morality of war, Birch defends his own integrity by stating: "These hands have spent years in toil, but not a moment in pilfering." As Birch makes this statement, Cooper writes that he is "stretching forth his meagre, bony fingers" so to further enhance Birch's common, salt of the earth persona.[45]

As the story unfolds, Cooper repeatedly idealizes Birch's work as a spy — for example having him turn down payment from George Washington near the novel's conclusion — even though Enoch Crosby, possibly the real life historical model for Cooper's Birch, was, in fact, paid.[46] In another section, despite the fact that the fictional Birch himself takes money for masterminding the escape of a British officer, Cooper dodges the moral reproaches attached to spying for pay and fortifies instead the connection between work, masculinity, and Christian rectitude in Birch's character.

But the stigma attached to the spy as the hero of a historical adventure was real and Cooper was well aware of the literary tradition into which he stepped. Accordingly — and perhaps in an effort to make

---

42 Ibid., 202.
43 McTiernan 1997.
44 Ibid.
45 Cooper 1997, 202.
46 The real life individuals Cooper used as sources for his characters have concerned several scholars. As early as 1823, it was claimed that David Gray, a Revolutionary War spy, was Cooper's model for Harvey Birch. In 1831, H. L. Barnum named Enoch Crosby as the prototype. This claim was disputed in two articles written in the 1890s by Guy Hatfield. Hatfield was promptly challenged by James Deane. More recently, Rufus Wilson and J. C. Pumpelly have supported the Crosby claim. Others continue to disagree, however, several of them putting forth their own candidates for the model. Tremaine McDowell takes issue with all of the above writers, claiming Birch was a product of Cooper's imagination. Against this backdrop, it seems that we may never really know which individual, if any, served as the model for Harvey Birch (Dyer 1991, xv).

Birch's character (and Cooper's own message) more effective — characters in the novel regularly speak against Cooper's ideological cleansing of espionage, muddying his portrayal of Birch by reiterating traditional censures. For example, in the novel, we find an American military judge expressing the conventional view in his rejection of Cooper's soldiers and spies analogy: "A soldier should never meet his enemy but openly. For fifty years have I served two kings of England, and now my native land; but never did I approach a foe, unless under the light of the sun, and with honest notice that an enemy was nigh."[47]

The period's aversion to spies is further articulated when Cooper allows the character of Birch to lament the reality of being a spy: "Yes, such are their laws; the man who fights, and kills, and plunders, is honoured; but he who serves his country as a spy, no matter how faithfully, no matter how honestly, lives to be reviled, or dies like the vilest criminal."[48] By including these passages, Cooper actively seeks to reflect the contemporary shame attached to spying not only by soldiers but by Anglo-American culture at large."[49] Most American reviews of *The Spy* reflected the general public revulsion of the spy being cast as a fictional hero.[50] One in particular pointedly stated: "No sympathy can be excited with meanness, and there must be a degree of meanness ever associated with the idea of the Spy. Neither poetry nor prose can ever make a spy a heroic character."[51]

Near the end of the novel, Cooper again employs nothing less than the person of George Washington — the symbolic "Father of the American Revolution" — to sum up the fate of the spy when Washington tells Birch: "There are many motives which might govern me, that to you are unknown. Our situations are different; I am known as the leader of armies — but you must descend into the grave with the reputation of

---

47 Cooper 1997, 302.

48 Ibid., 331.

49 McTiernan 1997.

50 In his bid to be granted a military pension, even Enoch Crosby himself appears to downplay his Revolutionary War espionage activities by emphasizing that he started as an enlisted man who fell into espionage only by chance, and resumed his career as a soldier after spending a mere nine months informing on loyalists. A facsimile of a later disposition indicates that Enoch Crosby received expense money as well as what he would have been paid if he had served as a soldier rather than a spy (Crosby 1975, 215).

51 Edgeworth 1967, 67.

a foe to your native land. Remember that the veil which conceals your true character cannot be raised in years — perhaps never."[52]

Still, while Cooper may allow Birch to defend his trade, and to receive praise from Washington for his "truth and principles," he never silences the accusations of other characters who consider Birch's behavior offensive. And it is this repetition that never allows the reader to forget that ordinary moral standards require the condemnation of Birch's behavior, no matter how often the narrator explicitly or implicitly absolves it. And herein lies perhaps the most singular of Cooper's accomplishments in *The Spy*. With Washington's words, Cooper has defined the fundamental premise that, even today, continues to run though espionage novels: the ambiguity of a neutral ground wherein secret men do secret things. Secondly, and notwithstanding the well entrenched social diagram of his time — one that considered spies to be liars, traitors, thieves or even worse — Cooper's fictional context raised public interest in espionage as a patriotic duty and, in some circles, facilitated the movement of espionage from the shadows and into the public forum.

While Cooper's treatments of "neutral ground" and "patriotic espionage" did, of course, endure the passage of time, what he did not seemingly accomplish was to generate any immediate literary succession, for it was some eighty years until the vague contours of a new literary genre were first suggested by two significant British works: Rudyard Kipling's *Kim* (1901), followed closely by Erskine Childers' *The Riddle of the Sands* (1903). The genre was to be termed "espionage fiction" and, through Kipling and Childers, we witness the beginning of the contemporary spy novel.

RUDYARD KIPLING -

> That the spy will fabricate his information is a mere commonplace. But in the sphere of political and revolutionary action, relying partly on violence, the professional spy has every facility to fabricate the very facts themselves, and will spread the double evil of emulation in one direction, and of panic, hasty legislation, unreflecting hate, in the other. However, this is an imperfect world.
>
> — Rudyard Kipling, *Kim*, 1901

---

52 Cooper, 398.

Rudyard Kipling (1865-1936) was a Nobel laureate who wrote novels, poems, and short stories, mostly set in India and Burma during the time of British rule. He was born in Bombay, India, and at age six was sent to be educated in England. Having written numerous other books including *The Jungle Book* (1894) and *Captains Courageous* (1897), Kipling's literary reputation was well established by the time he published *Kim* in 1901. It soon became one of the more enduring books of Britain's age of empire and typifies British imperialist literature of the late Victorian era. In the novel, Kipling details the fictional exploits of an Anglo-Indian orphan boy, *Kim*, who becomes a player in the shadowy but extensive system of British surveillance and espionage on the frontiers of India.

While some critics suggest that *Kim* is a somewhat marginal model of the traditionally heroic spy novel, it does offer certain evolutionary constructs to the genre primarily because it is based on a contradiction: it is an imperial novel that at the same time denies the Indian experience of colonialism.[53] In this, albeit urbane, sense, then, it emerges as not only a spy novel but a spy novel that is at the same time typical of English colonial novels in which English culture is depicted to be dominant and sacrosanct.[54]

In *Kim*, Kimball O'Hara, the orphaned son of an Irish soldier and a mother who died in childbirth, is taken in by a vagabond lama and recruited by the British military. Kim can "pass" for Indian. He is *chela*, or disciple to the lama, and sees no contradiction between this and spying for the British. Espionage is a game for Kim, and this game aspect effectively displaces questions of ethics and legitimacy to the realm of sportsmanship, while the specific function of the other, minor Indian characters is seemingly to ratify the legitimacy of English rule. *Kim* affirms the lama's conservative and rather innocent worldview and attempts to suppress the resistance of races, customs, caste cultures, and languages.[55]

---

53 Thompson 1993, 83.
54 More popular British colonial novels include *A Passage to India* (1924) by E.M. Forster, that contemplates the arrogance of British colonialism in India, and, to some extent, *Jane Eyre*(1846) by Charlotte Bronte, that has an interesting colonial connection through Rochester's Caribbean plantations and his mad Jamaican wife.
55 Thompson 1993, 87-89.

Similar to Cooper's *The Spy*, espionage in *Kim* is depicted as a form of patriotic adventure that places a premium on disguise, cleverness, and individual heroics. Cast against inept French and Russian spies, Kim proves to be a natural and nimble operative, but his exploits are aided and abetted by other native players, principally the Bengali clerk and a Pathan horse dealer. Such a supporting cast allowed Kipling to map and affirm the structures of British imperial control of India. But what Kipling fails to do in *Kim* is to incorporate any of the conflicts or resistances in India, preferring instead to openly support imperialism, in order to presumably remain in concert with British popular thought.[56] This aside, *Kim* does indeed seek to explore — at least conceptually — the more theoretical nuances of the heroic spy novel, therein anticipating the romantic and heroic traditions pursued by later espionage authors such as Buchan, Oppenheim, and Fleming.

Yet despite its heroic minimalism and heady invocation of empire, Kipling's *Kim* did tender a significant contribution to the genre. Primarily it gave to espionage fiction the suggestive pieces of a formula in which exotic locales, travelogue, heroic action, caricatured depiction of the enemy, and ultimately political affirmation could all be set to work. And it was a similar formula, albeit differently constituted, that Erskine Childers pursued in his only work of espionage fiction, *The Riddle of the Sands* (1903), wherein two Englishmen stumble upon and foil a vast German plan to mount a surprise naval assault on Great Britain.

---

56 Landrum 1999, 29.

CHAPTER 3. WORLD WAR I — EMPIRE AND ESPIONAGE

> War is not merely a political act, but also a real political instrument, a continuation of political commerce, a carrying out of the same by other means.
> — Prussian General Karl von Clausewitz, *On War*, 1832

The onset of the contemporary espionage novel emerged near the turn of the century, during the late 1890s and early 1900s, and with it one observes a marked shift in British popular fiction.[57] But this adjustment is certainly not unique in nature. On the contrary, it is but a minor element in the profound cultural transformation of the popular classes which occurred between the 1880s and the 1920s — a period of significant change spawned by Britain's move toward social imperialism.[58]

---

57 The adventure story was the dominant genre in the popular fiction for men in Victorian England, ranging from the boys' stories of Mayne Reid, G.A. Henry, and R.M. Ballantyne, to the tales of more established writers such as Charles Kingsley, H. Rider Haggard, and Robert Louis Stevenson (Denning 1987, 38).

58 *Social Imperialism* is a term used by a number of scholars during recent years. One of them, political scientist Franz Neumann, describes it as an attempt on the part of the governing classes to provide a mass base for imperialism, and to incorporate working classes into an imperialistic system in order to garner popular support for aggressive expansion. Economist J. A. Schumpeter takes another tack, defining it as an imperialism in which entrepreneurs seduced the workers with social welfare concessions, and, in fact, a thinly veiled attempt to revive the people's imperialisms of ancient times, to create a warrior nation modeled after the ancient Assyrians or the Arabs of the early Middle Ages (Semmel 1960, 13).

Most succinctly, in the British model, social imperialism was an attempt to expand the empire's material holdings — principally gold and diamonds — in South Africa, India and elsewhere in order to generate revenues that could then be applied to diminish domestic discontent through economic improvements and social reforms back in England. In the grander scheme of things, this was a critical time because in this period also lies the matrix of factors and problems from which our present history and our present dilemmas arise. Everything changes — not just a shift in the relations of forces but a reconstitution of the terrain of the geopolitical-economic struggle itself — and many of the characteristic forms of what we now think of as "traditional" popular culture either emerge from, or emerge in their distinctive modern form, during this period.[59] The impact on espionage fiction was significant, for it was this same reconstruction of geopolitical-economic terrain — particularly in relation to Britain's history of imperialism and empire — that facilitates the emergence of espionage as a viable fictional premise.

To preserve the financial wherewithal to continue economic and social programs at home, the empire, of course, had to be preserved, particularly with respect to its holdings abroad. This sense of protectionism manifested itself in a society-wide notion of "the enemy outside" and became one of the fundamental themes of British imperialist culture at the time. Empire was increasingly celebrated in school rooms, shops, and factories; and from pulpits and political platforms; there was Empire Day, a series of Colonial and Imperial Conferences, the imperial certainties expressed in the *Daily Mail* and other new, heavily subscribed dailies, and, ultimately, the widely accepted concept of an empire upon which the sun never set.[60]

As the spy novel reflects the times in which it is written, the "enemy outside" theme concurrently served to facilitate the transition from the assertive, confident, and expansionist themes of adventure fiction to the increasingly insular, even paranoid, espionage genre that stressed vigilance and protection against invasion.[61] Imperialism and imperialist culture was central to the genre's successful evolution and the spy

---

59 Hall 1981, 229.
60 Judd 1996, 11.
61 Blanch 1979, 119.

novel found a fertile ground in the public fears of invasion and of managing and resolving the invasion "crisis" in the popular imagination.[62] In reality, the public fears were not totally unfounded for, at the turn of century, there was indeed a decline of British imperialism and this, as could be expected, spawned the perception of Britain's waning political, economic and military preeminence both at home and abroad.

In the period leading up to World War I, there existed a complex series of strategic alliances among most European countries, as well as major economic and territorial rivalries among Great Britain, France and Germany resulting from their empire building in the last half of the nineteenth century. It was also a period marked by technological advances such as the internal combustion engine and the sharp upward curve of the destructiveness of improved weaponry. These new technologies and imperial rivalries brought about a quickening of tempo in international relations with an increased capacity and willingness to wage war.

While most major European powers accepted these technological advancements with some reluctance, the German military embraced them, and their professional general staff integrated technology into a military doctrine centered around scholarly research, meticulously detailed planning and a thorough indoctrination in a logical concept of war.[63] Further, this integration had, by the late nineteenth century, successfully manifested itself in the Prussian victories over Austria (1866) and France (1871), thus causing Prussia to be acknowledged as the leading land military power of the world, a position that Prussia still held at the beginning of the twentieth century.

In marked contrast to Prussian doctrine, Britain's military had long resisted the introduction of a general staff system and other interrelated reforms because to many people in Britain this appeared to be a step toward militarism. But embarrassing evidence of military inefficiency drawn from Britain's efforts in the second Boer War (1902) clearly indicated that the British military was unprepared to counter any national security threat. To deal with this lack of preparation, numerous agencies within the British military establishment, as well as special inqui-

---

62 Denning 1987, 38.
63 Dupuy 1986, 821.

ries — those of the Esher Committee and Lord Richard Haldane held particular influence — moved to resolve the problem.

Yet even as these formal evaluations were proceeding, a previously unknown writer, Erskine Childers, himself a British veteran of the Boer War in South Africa, published a solitary espionage novel, *The Riddle of the Sands* (1903). Its publication held twofold significance: First and foremost, it brought to the attention of the general public the troubles of Britain's dwindling military capability; but, secondly, by embracing the proposal of plots and themes being set astride existing geopolitical scenarios, it marked the advent of the modern spy novel.

Erskine Childers -

> By God, I'll give you five minutes to be off to England and be damned to you, or else to be locked up for spies!
> — Erskine Childers, *Riddle of the Sands*, 1903

Erskine Childers (1870-1922) was born in England and educated at Trinity College, Cambridge. He worked as a clerk in the House of Commons and was one of the first volunteers accepted for service in the Boer War. In 1903, Childers published *The Riddle of the Sands: A Record of Secret Service Recently Achieved*, a narrative of yachting and espionage off the northwest coast of Germany. In a historical sense, Cooper and Kipling aside, *Riddle of the Sands* is generally considered to be the first work of modern spy fiction, a distinction drawn primarily from Childers' experimentation with the deceptive blending of fact and fiction.

Written in 1902, the story concerns two young Englishmen who make a trip to the Frisian Islands and discover the Germans rehearsing plans for an invasion of Britain. Carruthers, a Foreign Office man with foppish mannerisms, is in the best tradition of the English amateur confronted with a difficult and dangerous situation, and his friend Davies is the foil. The villain is a former British naval lieutenant named Dollmann who has turned traitor and is working for the Germans. Perhaps some of the best narrative is that concerning the navigation of their seven-ton yacht *Dulcibella* in a fog through the waters off the German Frisian Islands.[64]

---

64 McCormick 1977, 46-47.

The story's factual basis was the result of Childers' own sailing experiences in the yacht *Vixen* off the coasts of Germany, Holland and elsewhere. It was fiction based on fact, but fiction with a set purpose: that of arousing public opinion in support of a stronger British navy. *The Riddle of the Sands* immediately became famous because, apart from being a rousing story, it drew attention to German militarism at a time when nobody else had taken up the theme. It was undoubtedly a patriotic gesture on the part of Childers, for his whole career suggests that he was as devoted to protecting England.[65]

One of the most striking things about *The Riddle of the Sands* is the resemblance to modern spy fiction, particularly with respect to the novel's technical facets. Childers describes the philosophy, theory, and practice of inshore sailing in exceptional detail; and the geographical structure around which the novel is built — the Baltic coast of Denmark and Schleswig-Holstein and the low-lying sandy coast between the Elbe and the Ems Rivers — is so accurate that the course taken by the two English heroes could be followed by any skilled yachtsman. If this were not enough, Childers even included maps to help the reader, together with timetables of tides. And while writers of contemporary espionage spy fiction follow this pattern of providing expert technical background, they rarely do so with the degree of knowledge and skill Childers commanded.[66]

The book also precipitated significant changes in the somewhat dilatory British Naval Intelligence Division. After being alerted to shortcomings in their naval charts, naval intelligence gave permission to two officers to be sent on a tour of the German seacoast defenses and the Frisian Islands. The officers found that the existing Admiralty charts of this area — as well as any general intelligence information on the locale — were hopelessly out of date and, in fact, their only real knowledge of the area was that obtained from *The Riddle of the Sands*. The two officers were both detected and arrested by the Germans, finally being sentenced to a term of imprisonment in Germany.[67]

---

65 Ibid.
66 Ibid.
67 The two officers were released in May 1913, seventeen months before the expiration of their terms.

Aside from being a rousing tale for the times, *The Riddle of the Sands* went straight to the heart of the British public's fear of invasion. Too, it is a remarkable example of the power of propaganda in fictional form — not only did the novel provide entertainment, but it also made members of the public and the British Government aware of a problem which was rectified as a result.[68] After Childers' death, the literary impact of *The Riddle of the Sands*, particularly the experiment of blending fact and fiction, continued to gain in popularity, with "faction" — as the deceptive blending of fact and fiction has come to be known — becoming the most significant trend in twentieth century espionage fiction.

With the widespread acceptance of *Kim* and *Riddle of the Sands*, the political and imaginative work of espionage fiction had begun on two principal fronts: Kipling equated espionage with imperial security, while Childers made the link between espionage and individual and national regeneration. In England, two writers saw the potential of what Kipling and Childers had begun and moved quickly to further refine the genre with respect to its commercial potential, as well as its reliance upon world military and geopolitical events. In reality, Edward Phillips Oppenheim and William Le Queux were men of similar and — some might say — modest literary talent; but, together, their influence upon the evolution of the spy novel was significant. Oppenheim and Le Queux became the first writers of mass-produced espionage fiction, and, without them, perhaps the single espionage novels of Kipling and Childers would have never captured such a wide audience.

EDWARD PHILLIPS OPPENHEIM ~

> You are a very youthful diplomat, Dicky, but even you have probably heard of governments who employ private messengers to carry dispatches which for various reasons they don't care to put through their embassies.
> — E. Phillips Oppenheim, *The Illustrious Prince*, 1910

Edward Phillips Oppenheim (1866-1946) began his writing career in 1882, a decade before Le Queux, and was a prolific writer, altogether turning out no less than 15 novels and 39 books of short stories — but,

---

68 McCormick and Fletcher 1990, 52.

as most critics agree, never a polished one.[69] In 1887, his first novel, *Expiation*, was published. On the strength of this, Oppenheim was able to secure a contract to write six serial stories for the *Sheffield Weekly Telegraph.*

Oppenheim was fascinated by the world of spies and secret diplomacy and set out not merely to explore it but to use it as a background for his fiction. In 1898, *The Mysterious Mr. Sabin* was published. He described this as "the first of my long series of stories dealing with that shadowy and mysterious world of diplomacy...So long as the world lasts, its secret international history will continue to engage the full activities of the diplomatist."[70] Oppenheim's stories were the Edwardian version of spy fiction, a mixture of romance, adventure, espionage, secret diplomacy and high life, intermingled with criminal activities and gambling in the world's greatest cities, Budapest and Vienna being two of his favorite settings. Eventually he personally gravitated toward other colorful European cities and resorts and thus added some first-hand knowledge to his work. Monte Carlo then became a favorite setting for his spy stories, notably *Mr. Grex of Monte Carlo* (1915). Oppenheim loved the good things of life and had a zest for exploring the capitals of Europe.[71]

Like William Le Queux and Erskine Childers, though to a lesser extent, Oppenheim became one of a small band of writers deeply concerned about what in the early 1900s was known as "the German menace." And it was the growing apprehension of the German threat to Britain in the years before 1914 that helped concentrate Oppenheim's mind and set his fiction firmly in the espionage genre. In novels like *The Maker of History* (1905) and *The Great Secret* (1907), amateur British agents uncover reprehensible German plots designed to fulfill a German lust for power and conquest at the expense of Britain and its newfound ally France. *The Great Secret* exposes a German spy ring some thirty thousand strong operating in Britain under the innocent guise of the Waiters Union and preparing to wreak havoc in support of an invasion of the British Isles.

---

69 Ibid., 204.
70 Oppenheim 1977, 144.
71 Standish 1957, 182.

With the outbreak of war in Europe in 1914, Oppenheim immediately volunteered for duty with the British Secret Intelligence Service, only to have his application rejected. But Oppenheim repressed his disappointment and, during World War I, he was employed escorting journalists of neutral countries on tours of the battlefront in France. It was during this period that, exploiting the war-charged themes of loyalty and power, he wrote the best of his espionage novels, availing himself of the popular mood of spy fever and anti-German hysteria stirred up by the sinking of the passenger liner *Lusitania in* May 1915.[72]

In 1916, Oppenheim published *Kingdom of the Blind*, a story that incorporated all manner of animated adventures, including German submarine attacks and Zeppelin raids, and also purported to reveal something of the methods of secret service operators. Oppenheim followed this up with *Pawns Count* (1918), another Germany spy tale which opens, like so many of Oppenheim's narratives, in a fashionable London restaurant where John Lutchester, of the British Secret Service, Oscar Fischer, a German American, and a beautiful New York girl, Pamela Van Teyl, are interested in securing the formula of a new explosive.

Oppenheim's wartime novels played on many of the then new — and now familiar — conventions of espionage fiction: a sinister conspiracy, the heroic work of a lone agent, and fast-paced action. Nevertheless, what really gave his novels their standing was the psychological attunement to the spirit of the day and, in particular, the sense that Britain's fortunes were fragile and were relentlessly being undermined by evil forces operating from within. Oppenheim's stories were commercially successful and shortly after World War I, he began to financially profit from his books, many of them being serialized in America in journals like *Colliers* and the *Saturday Evening Post*. But soon, even though he had an earlier start, the prolific Oppenheim eventually found himself overtaken by an even more prolific espionage novelist: the writer whose publishers christened "The Master of Mystery" — William Le Queux.[73]

---

72 Wark 1998, 1201.
73 Publishers Hodder & Stoughton emblazoned this banner headline on many Le Queux books.

WILLIAM TUFNELL LE QUEUX ~

> After crossing the frontier, you will assume the name of
> Count de Bourbriac, and Valentine will pass as the Countess.
> A suitable suite of rooms have been taken for you at the Grand
> Hotel Brussels, where you will find your luggage on your arrival.
> Mademoiselle will supply you with funds. I shall be in Brussels,
> but shall not approach you.
> — William Le Queux, *The Story of a Secret*, 1906

William Tufnell Le Queux (1864-1927) was born in London, but
his early life seems to have been spent traveling about Europe with his
parents, resulting in a somewhat indiscriminate private education in
England, Italy and France. For a time, Le Queux studied art in Paris
and lived in the Latin Quarter, but wanderlust caused him to abandon
a career in painting to tour France and Germany on foot. During these
travels, he accumulated a vast amount of information, especially material concerning military history and current affairs.[74]

On little more than the experience of drifting aimlessly around Europe, Le Queux became a journalist and was a roving correspondent
until 1891, when he was appointed foreign editor of London's *Globe*
newspaper. This post was given to him because of a series of articles he
had written for *The Times* about the revolutionary movement in Russia.
However, Le Queux was gifted with a spirited imagination and, while
appropriate for a novelist, it eventually ruined his journalistic endeavors. He developed a reputation for being an unreliable witness who was
given to extravagant embellishment of a situation, sometimes present-
ing downright fiction as fact. By 1893, Le Queux had resigned his edi-
torship to spend all his time writing books, of which he produced more
than a hundred during his lifetime.[75]

Le Queux's first novel, *Guilty Bonds* (1895), was based upon his travels in Russia — where it was subsequently banned — and involved political intrigue, a theme that was to continue. He moved closer still to
espionage fiction in novels like *The Great War in England in 1897* (1894), a
Russo-French plot for the invasion of England; and *England's Peril* (1899),
that introduced the villainous Gaston La Touche, chief of the French

---

74 McCormick and Fletcher 1990, 159.
75 Ibid.

Secret Service. Le Queux doubtless realized the popularity — and attendant personal profitability — of the invasion theme and continued to exploit various scenarios. This was particularly true in *The Invasion of 1910* (1906), which also offered Le Queux his first real measure of fame. In fact, this novel was little more than a propaganda broadsheet, as it depicted a small force of German spies undertaking sabotage in Britain in preparation for the much larger invasion of the thinly disguised "Nordener" army that would overrun and perfunctorily destroy the English homeland. In book form, *The Invasion of 1910* sold more than one million copies in twenty-seven languages, but there were other, more important, results.[76] Le Queux realized that he was on to something. He had found a way in which he could alert Britain to the danger from Germany and, at the same time, turn a handsome profit on the book sales. From this moment on, the two motives — patriotism and pounds sterling — became inextricably mixed in Le Queux's mind.[77]

Spies of the Kaiser (1909), Le Queux's next novel, teemed with authentic and, if not actual evidence, at least well researched incidental detail, and chronicled the discovery of all manner of German espionage activities ranging from surveillance of England's coastal defenses to attempted thefts of plans for advanced battleships, submarines and airplanes. To lend further credibility to the narrative, Le Queux noted in the introduction: "As I write, I have before me a file of amazing documents, which plainly show the feverish activity with which this advance guard of our enemy is working."

While it is virtually certain that Le Queux possessed no such documents — as none, save his own, seemingly existed — *Spies of the Kaiser* nonetheless achieved the desired effect. Soon after its publication Le Queux began to receive letters detailing the suspicious behavior of German waiters, barbers and tourists in the vicinity of telephone, telegraph, bridges and railway lines on the east coast and around London. While the various reports presented what amounted to be little more than the amplification of *Spies of the Kaiser*'s fictional scenarios, Le

---

76 When Le Queux's *Invasion of 1910* was translated into German — as *Der Einfall der Deutschen in England* — the editor left out the last two hundred pages, which described how the British counter-attacked against the invading Germans and massacred them in the streets of London (Hewitson 2004, 95).
77 Knightly 1986, 15-16.

Queux considered them to be even more proof of Germany's malicious intentions and, more to the point, independent confirmation of his own suspicions. With letters in hand, Le Queux sought to elevate his own "spy catcher" reputation by sharing them with the British government. His point of contact was his friend Lieutenant Colonel (later Brigadier General Sir) James Edmonds, then director of MO5 which addressed military counterintelligence operations. While Edmonds' job was to uncover foreign spies in Britain, in fact, he did nothing of the sort. However, in fairness, this cannot be attributed to a lack of will or skill — he later authored Britain's official history of World War I on the Western Front — but rather to his negligible £200 annual budget and the fact that his entire staff consisted of but two assistants.[78]

At what can only be viewed as a magical moment in history, Le Queux's new evidence reached Edmonds at precisely the right moment. Besieged by the onslaught of public opinion, rumor and outright lies — much of it spawned by Le Queux's own incendiary novels — Edmonds found himself facing a situation wherein the specter of a German invasion, however improbable, had been all but legitimized. For Edmonds, this was an impossible situation. As the one official charged with discovering German espionage activities in England, he had, in reality, no proof whatsoever. Yet, wise in the ways of government — and with an eye to his own budget and staffing levels — he took his "conclusions" to R. B. Haldane, the secretary of state for war, who, in March 1909, directed the Committee of Imperial Defence to examine "the nature and extent of the foreign espionage that is at present taking place within this country and the danger to which it may expose us." Chaired by Lord Haldane himself, the membership was impressive, an indication of how seriously the government regarded the subject. Included were the First Lord of the Admiralty, the Home Secretary, the permanent undersecretaries of the Treasury and the Foreign Office, the Commissioner of Metropolitan Police, the Director of Military Operations, and the Director of Naval Intelligence.

There is little doubt that both Colonel Edmonds and Le Queux legitimately believed Britain to be in deadly peril from German ambition and were convinced that a German spy network was already es-

---

78 Matin 1999.

tablished and at work throughout the country. To this end, Edmonds presented to the committee a variety of evidentiary documentation concerning German espionage in Britain, much of it misinterpreted or fabricated by himself and Le Queux. The committee routinely accepted Edmond's arguments, releasing a statement that the evidence left no reservation in the minds of the committee but that an extensive system of German espionage existed in Britain, and that the British government had no organization for keeping in touch with that espionage and for accurately determining its extent or objectives.[79]

In 1914, *The Invasion of 1910* was made into a film that depicted the executions of captured members of the English opposition at Beccles, in Suffolk, and the last stand of the British Army at Maldon, in Essex, where their central position was defended by the trenches and barbed wire entanglements that would soon become so familiar during World War I. The film was submitted to the British Board of Film Censors as *The Raid of 1915* and was rejected as offensive to a foreign power; however, when war was declared, it was hurriedly released under its new title, *If England Were Invaded.*

When war actually began, Le Queux continued the same theme in such books as *The Mystery of the Green Ray* (1915), *Number 70 Berlin* (1916), and *The Zeppelin Destroyer* (1916). But with each successive story, he tended to make his plots increasingly preposterous, though admittedly some of the background detail was authentic. In some sense it appears that Le Queux, too, was a casualty of the war, although from a literary point of view, for he became so obsessed with the war that it robbed his writing of any remaining objectivity or detachment. Still, William Le Queux certainly remains one of the earliest writers of espionage fiction proper and he established a distinct pattern for the genre. Though his warnings of Britain's lack of preparation to face a continental invasion had none of the literary quality of Erskine Childers, his sheer sensationalism and journalistic sense for the topical made his novels potent propaganda that reached a huge readership and held sway over public opinion for nearly a decade.[80]

---

79 Knightly 1986, 19.
80 England was certainly not alone in her suspicions of Germany. Violations of American neutrality gradually helped to convince American policy makers that it too was being attacked from within. Though German intrigue in the United

JOSEPH CONRAD ~

> Some reason, you understand, I mean some sense, may creep
> into thinking; some glimpse of truth. I mean some effective truth,
> for which there is no room in politics or journalism.
> — Joseph Conrad, *Nostromo*, 1904

While Le Queux and Oppenheim continued to mass produce their
pulp spy novels, Joseph Conrad (1857-1924) was already achieving
some measure of literary fame with early works such as *The Nigger of the
Narcissus* (1897), *Lord Jim* (1900), and the novellas *Youth* (1902), *Heart of
Darkness* (1902), and *Typhoon* (1903). But the unsophisticated politics of
Le Queux's and Oppenheim's prewar fiction, however profitable, were
certainly not those of Conrad, who was more interested in probing another area of international politics — terrorism and revolution — than
in telling stories of questionable German espionage plots.

Like his contemporaries, Conrad also embraced world political
events as backdrops to his novels, but his characters were considerably
more complex. They were generally outsiders — as he himself was —
and more fully developed, both psychologically and emotionally.[81] In
this light, Conrad is viewed as more than an espionage novelist. Better
put, he was a "political" novelist skirting the periphery of the espionage genre wherein he offered dark portrayals of political intrigue and
betrayal, and of the ceaseless but, in Conrad's eyes, futile espionage between countries.[82]

By the end of the nineteenth century, the spy was not only attract-
ing the attention of dime novelists and other writers of popular adventure but of serious novelists as well. Dostoyevsky had used the theme
of clandestine affairs in several of his novels, but it was Joseph Conrad

---

States eventually waned upon America's entry into the war, anti-German hysteria continued to rise. In 1918 the craze culminated with the lynching of Robert
Prager, an alien unjustly accused of espionage. Many sources fueled the nation's
anxiety. The German government's actions and the exposure of such actions
in the press alarmed the public. Additionally, in the period 1914 to 1917, many
German-American institutions and organizations were so strident in their support of the Kaiser as to appear ambiguous in their loyalties. American political
leaders and private preparedness organizations vocalized and exacerbated public concerns about German spies (McDonnell 1995, 21).
81 Bancroft 1964, 23.
82 Cawelti and Rosenberg 1987, 39.

who first created — in *The Secret Agent* (1907) — a modern tragedy with espionage as its central theme. It was a major step forward in the development of the genre.[83]

Joseph Conrad was born Josef Teodor Konrad Korzeniowski, the only child of Polish parents in the Russian-controlled Ukraine. Orphaned as a child, he became a ward of his maternal uncle and, when he was sixteen years old, he left Poland, destined for France. He led an adventurous life during this time: he worked on ships running guns; he entered the merchant service of England; and he became a British citizen in 1886 and traveled extensively in exotic locales such as the Malay Archipelago and the Congo River. Conrad spoke four languages — Russian, Polish, French, and English — and, doubtlessly drawing from his life experiences, was a skilled creator of atmosphere, realism, drama, and symbolism.

In the most fundamental sense, Conrad viewed society as a criminal conspiracy and his characters frequently have some negative epiphany in which self and world dissolve into script, stage set, and lighting.[84] Moreover, beginning with his publication of *The Secret Agent*, Conrad invented a new form or, more specifically, a new approach to the world of clandestine affairs. The detective novel had existed since the nineteenth century in the work of Dickens, Dostoyevsky, and Arthur Conan Doyle, but Conrad revised the detective novel by joining to it political events, individual conspiratorial acts, and ideology, giving us for the first time, surely in English, the political-detective novel. Here we have something of the suspense and mystery associated with the detective novel linked to materials that seem quite distinct. Obviously, this linkage raises the genre's sophistication, for the introduction of political ideas means that the detective novel is no longer simply a work of narrative mystery but one of ideas and conflicting ideologies. The result is a political thriller that also becomes a moral tale. The chief beneficiary of this kind of novel is Graham Greene, but before him novelists as diverse as Thomas Mann and Andre Malraux were deeply influenced by Conrad's "invention."[85]

---

83 Ibid.
84 Hilfer 1990, 98.
85 Karl 1983, 9.

Conrad crafted *The Secret Agent* from the seed of an actual attempt, made in 1894, to blow up the Greenwich Observatory. But Conrad expands on the Greenwich affair and turns his eye to the world of law and order, fatuous civil servants, corrupt policemen and squalid terrorist landscapes.[86] It concerns a group of spies and anarchists who meet in the Soho shop of Verloc, and Verloc's wife Winnie, who married him mainly to look after her marginally retarded younger brother Stevie.[87]

Verloc, who sells mostly pornographic items in his shop, actually receives most of his income by supplying information to an unnamed foreign embassy. As Verloc is part of a loose circle of anarchists and revolutionaries, he reports on their activities to both the embassy and to the London police. Settled and comfortable in this unconventional lifestyle, he becomes distraught when he visits the embassy and finds he has a new control officer, one who wants not information but action and who is willing to terminate his employment unless some action is seen. Other figures in Verloc's band of anarchists are Ossipon, who makes money from seducing women, and "the Professor," an American

---

86 Conrad's novel, published in 1907, provides a fictional explanation for the explosion at Greenwich Observatory on 15 February 1894. The accidental bombing was caused by one Martial Bourdin, who was severely injured in the blast and died a few days later, but without having revealed his motivation or his political connections, if any. In fact, investigations at the time soon revealed that Bourdin had a number of connections to anarchism. He had been a member of the French section of the anarchist *Autonomie* Club after his immigration to London. Earlier, in Paris, he had associated with a society of tailors — Bourdin was by profession a ladies' tailor — called "*L'Aiguille*" (The Needle) that was largely anarchist. However, most important for Conrad's purposes, he was the brother-in-law of H. B. Samuels, publisher of the anarchist journal *Commonweal*. This last detail is significant because another London anarchist, David Nicoll, was jealous of Samuels's position in *Commonweal* and used the Greenwich episode to cast doubts on Samuels's loyalty to the cause. In Nicoll's version of events, published as the *Greenwich Mystery* in 1897, Bourdin is portrayed as an obedient simpleton "looking into his [Samuels'] eyes with loving trust," while Samuels is said to be in the pay of the police. Neither assertion about the character of the two men is corroborated elsewhere, but Nicoll's account was taken up by Conrad in his story of the trusting idiot Stevie, and the self-serving police spy Verloc. In truth, Bourdin and Samuels can hardly be said to have collaborated at all in bringing about the bombing. Further, there was no reason to believe the observatory itself had been targeted at all: Bourdin may have been delivering the explosives to someone else, or may have been attempting to hide them for later use (Weir 1997, 74-75).

87 Bernstein 2003.

terrorist who walks the streets with a bomb strapped to his chest so he presumably will never be captured alive.[88]

Largely this is a comedy of errors, and we see the almost absurd ruin of Verloc, who takes on a ridiculously ambitious terrorist job to blow up the Greenwich Observatory. He compels his naïve brother-in-law Stevie to plant the bomb, but the boy is blown up and Winnie, learning of her brother's death, murders Verloc. She plans to leave the country with Ossipon but inevitably all goes wrong and she commits suicide. The story itself is characteristically Conrad — dark and sardonic — but it also seems to illustrate Conrad's suspicion about the worth of radical politics and anarchism.

Conrad's next political novel, *Under Western Eyes* (1911), is set in Czarist Russia and Geneva, astride the complex historical, social, and psychological climate of Russia shortly before the Bolshevik revolution. In *Under Western Eyes*, Conrad becomes the first serious writer to deal effectively with the double-agent. But it could be said that Conrad was writing with ardent sincerity and seriousness rather than to entertain, for his spies were not characters intended to amuse, but were symbols of what Conrad regarded as the essential evil of revolution. Cast against a broad canvas of political repression and revolt, *Under Western Eyes* involves assassins and émigré revolutionaries and their clandestine infiltration by a government spy. There are two narrators: Razumov, the student who becomes a reluctant spy after he betrays the idealistic Haldin to the authorities — Haldin is subsequently hanged — and an unnamed British teacher of languages, who watches the strange activities of the revolutionary exiles with the *Western eyes* of the title. He is calm, liberal and rational, everything that the Russians are not.[89] Razumov is attending St. Petersburg University, preparing himself for a career in the czarist bureaucracy, and suddenly finds himself ensnared in a secret plot when the radical Haldin assassinates a senior Russian government official.[90]

While *Under Western Eyes* is indeed a somber story, and darkly pessimistic, Conrad adroitly explores the concealments, intrigues and be-

---

88 Ibid.
89 Cowley 1998.
90 Long 2003.

trayals of czarist Russia's political turbulence, as well the psychological repercussions drawn from its endemic violence and oppression.[91] No one emerges victorious from his or her struggles, and everyone is morally compromised. Razumov, a reactionary, despises the revolutionaries with whom he mingles, and yet, even as he betrays Haldin, he expresses admiration for the young assassin's vigor and lofty daring.[92] Razumov believes in nothing, not even in Russia, a vast snow-covered country Conrad describes as a "monstrous blank page awaiting the record of an inconceivable history."[93] The only thing left open to him — the only thing that Razumov believes will release him from his "prison of lies" — is to tell the revolutionaries of his duplicity in the betrayal of Haldin. He confesses to another revolutionary who, unbeknownst to Razumov, is yet another double agent working for Razumov's own controller, therein completing the circle of deceit and duplicity.[94]

Conrad's Russia is cast as a country on the edge of neurosis, moving toward complete moral collapse: a corrupt, autocratic society composed of immoral individuals who suffer perpetual indignation and who can find no release for their ambitions.[95] Moreover, there is no small measure of historical accuracy in the novel, which deftly depicts the political turmoil in 1911 Czarist Russia. Still, there remains a handful of critics that continue to suggest that *The Secret Agent* and *Under Western Eyes* should not be described as spy novels. Alternatively, others feel Conrad must be considered as an indispensable contributor to espionage fiction, due to geopolitical accuracy of his settings and background ma-

---

91 Andreas 1959, 87.

92 Cowley 1998.

93 Conrad 2001.

94 In an intriguing departure from the norm, Greaney notes that while espionage and political violence are as central to *Under Western Eyes* as they were to *The Secret Agent*; the novels also share a decidedly edgy relationship with the reader. But in terms of its representation of language and human subjectivity, *Under Western Eyes* might be read as a brutally unsentimental rewriting of *Lord Jim*. Razumov, the novel's studiously innocuous hero, commits a grievous betrayal of trust and is pursued from St Petersburg to Geneva by compromising rumors and echoes of his guilt. Thus, the St Petersburg/Geneva dichotomy superficially resembles the Patna/Patusan split in *Lord Jim*; but for Razumov there is no Patusan, no compensatory linguistic utopia, no Jim-like martyrdom — only a final deafness that functions both as a sadistic "remedy" for his fear of words and as a violent caricature of the general reader's own "deafness" to the finer nuances of Conrad's prose (Greaney 2001, 152).

95 Cowley 1998.

terial — a most unusual characteristic in the days of Oppenheim and Le Queux — and because of his development of the double-agent as a viable fictional character.[96] Accordingly, drawn primarily from this engagement with real world geopolitics, and reinforced by his insights into the fundamental tradecraft of espionage, Conrad anticipates the path taken by Somerset Maugham, Graham Greene, Eric Ambler, and John Le Carré, and thus emerges as a central figure in the evolution of the genre.[97]

G.K. CHESTERTON —

> An anarchist is an artist. The man who throws a bomb is an artist, because he prefers a great moment to everything. He sees how much more valuable is one burst of blazing light, one peal of perfect thunder, than the mere common bodies of a few shapeless policemen. An artist disregards all governments, abolishes all conventions.
> — G.K. Chesterton, *The Man Who Was Thursday*, 1908

Journalist, essayist, poet, critic, broadcaster, and novelist, Gilbert Keith Chesterton (1874-1936) is probably best remembered for his detective stories, particularly those featuring the fictional Essex priest-detective Father Brown, who was based on his close friend Father John O'Connor. O'Connor was the parish priest of a church in Bradford, who in 1922 received Chesterton into the Roman Catholic Church. During his thirty-five-year writing career, Chesterton published nearly one hundred books, contributed to two hundred more, and wrote thousands of articles and poems for over a dozen periodicals. He was an optimistic man with a love of paradox and whimsy who, in 1908, penned a lone spy story, *The Man Who Was Thursday: A Nightmare* — an exploration of double agentry and the futility of espionage. Like Conrad, Chesterton declined to exploit the popularity of the "German" menace, preferring instead to draw on the fears of anarchist conspiracies and bomb outrages that prevailed in turn of the century London.[98]

---

96 McCormick and Fletcher 1990, 61.
97 Landrum 1999, 30.
98 Tibbets 1998, 181.

Some genre aficionados feel that Chesterton's *The Man Who Was Thursday* is the best spy novel ever written. And while, at first glance, it might seems a parody of the average spy novel, upon closer inspection it emerges as something considerably more than satire for it contains a deep-lying truth: if an agent says quite openly that he is a spy or an anarchist, no one will believe him and he will be able to do pretty much as he pleases. Attempts to hide one's identity leads to suspicion, and then everyone will know he is a spy (or an anarchist). In recent years, especially since the Bond era, there have been some attempts to satirize the spy novel but most of them have been heavy-handed compared with Chesterton's subtle little masterwork.[99]

Born in London, Chesterton studied English literature at London University. During the Boer War, he took a pro-Boer stand on the platform and in his writing. Between 1900 and 1910, he turned out numerous essays touching on political, philosophical, literary and other topics, and reveling in fierce but friendly debate. Chesterton's first attempt at fiction was *The Club of Queer Trades* (1905), a half-parody of Sherlock Holmes stories. This was followed three years later by the more widely regarded *The Man Who Was Thursday*, which became his central contribution to the evolution of the genre.

The Man Who Was Thursday begins with Gabriel Syme, a policeman posing as an anarchist poet. The purpose of the guise is an attempt to meet real anarchists and, if possible, to infiltrate their ranks. Syme succeeds to an extent that he never would have dreamed possible — he is elected to the position of "Thursday" in The Council of Days, the highest anarchist council, in which each member is known by a day of the week. Chesterton's approach to this espionage scenario is unique. When Syme is shown into the steel chamber of the underground movement, Chesterton makes no effort to detail weaponry in the manner upon which contemporary espionage novelists rely.[100] He simply observes that "there were no rifles or pistols in this apartment, but round the walls of it were hung more dubious and dreadful shapes, things that

---

99 Atkins 1984, 265.
100 McCormick and Fletcher 1990, 49.

looked like the bulbs of iron plants, or the eggs of iron birds. They were bombs, and the very room itself seemed like the inside of a bomb."[101]

Chesterton, in an age when the double-agent was almost unheard of in fact — except perhaps in Conrad's Czarist Russia — anticipates a scenario more frequently employed in later espionage novels: two rival agents who have exchanged confidences confronting one another. And, in this instance, after a series of such confrontations, it is Syme who discovers that the other council members are, in reality, also detectives; but, too, real anarchists. When Syme is discovered, he is confronted by Lucian Gregory — another council member — who is holding Syme at gunpoint.[102] The resolution is a classic scene that has played out in dozens of double-agent espionage stories in the years since Chesterton:

> "Don't be such a silly man," he [Syme] said, with the effeminate dignity of a curate. "Don't you see it's not necessary? Don't you see that we're both in the same boat? Yes, and jolly sea-sick."
>
> Gregory could not speak, but he could not fire either, and he looked his question.
>
> "Don't you see we've checkmated each other?" cried Syme. "I can't tell the police you are an anarchist. You can't tell the anarchists I'm a policeman. I can only watch you, knowing what you are; you can only watch me, knowing what I am. In short, it's a lonely, intellectual duel, my head against yours. I'm a policeman deprived of the help of the police. You, my poor fellow, are an anarchist deprived of the help of that law and organization which is so essential to anarchy. The one solitary difference is in your favour. You are not surrounded by inquisitive policemen; I am surrounded by inquisitive anarchists. I cannot betray you, but I might betray myself. Come, come: wait and see me betray myself. I shall do it so nicely."
>
> Gregory put the pistol slowly down, still staring at Syme as if he were a sea-monster. "I don't believe in immortality," he said at last, "but if, after all this, you were to break your word, God would make a hell only for you, to howl in forever."
>
> "I shall not break my word," said Syme sternly, "nor will you break yours."[103]

There was a romanticism about Chesterton's approach not only to the detective story but to the espionage genre as well, a lifting of the genre to a level of what can perhaps be called an "esoteric fantasy,"

101 Chesterton 1986, 22.
102 McCormick and Fletcher 1990, 50.
103 Chesterton 1986, 29.

which is one of the primary features of *The Man Who Was Thursday*. Further, Chesterton's attitude toward espionage fiction — contrasted to that of Oppenheim or Le Queux — is more directed to the romance of man, as opposed to the patriotism of empire.[104] Chesterton himself perhaps put it most succinctly when he wrote:

> No one can have failed to notice that in these stories the hero or the investigator crosses London with something of the loneliness and liberty of a prince in a tale of elfland, that in the course of that incalculable journey the casual omnibus assumes the primal colours of a fairy ship. The lights of the city begin to glow like innumerable goblin eyes, since they are the guardians of some secret, however crude, which the writer knows and the reader does not. Every twist of the road is like a finger pointing to it; every fantastic skyline of chimney pots seems wildly and derisively signaling the meaning of the mystery.[105]

There has been considerable debate over the underlying meaning of *The Man Who Was Thursday*, the vast majority of it academic and esoteric and heavily laden with religious connotation. Some critics argue that it can be interpreted in terms of Chesterton's sacramental view of life, according to which nature conceals and leads to the divine.[106] Others suggest Gabriel Syme personifies some sort of God-seeker and holy fool — like Job and Christ — a policeman bearing the name of an angel who reaches the limits of logic as he confronts the undecipherable riddle of life. While these interpretations may sound thoughtful and insightful, Chesterton himself declared another, seemingly darker, objective in his own foreword to *The Man Who Was Thursday: A Play in Three Acts* (1926): "I was not then considering whether anything is really evil, but whether everything is evil."[107]

So while it proves difficult to define the underlying meaning of *The Man Who Was Thursday*, it is possible to say that it is a classic spy novel that possesses many elements in common with contemporary espionage fiction: intrigues, secret plots, nefarious activity, and an enterprising hero. It is also believable, while at the same time retaining a sense of mystery heightened by glimpses of the ordinary world against which

---

104 McCormick and Fletcher 1990, 49.
105 Chesterton 1901.
106 Boyd 1975, 44.
107 Tibbetts 1988 192.

the drama unfolds. In the end, *The Man Who Was Thursday* anticipates almost every spy story that was ever written and remains a model for aspiring writers of espionage fiction, a textbook of sorts to keep them from drifting too far in the direction of fantasy.[108]

JOHN BUCHAN ~

> There's some nasty business afoot, and he found out too much and lost his life over it. But I am ready to take my oath that it is ordinary spy work. A certain great European Power makes a hobby of her spy system, and her methods are not too particular. Since she pays by piecework her blackguards are not likely to stick at a murder or two. They want our naval dispositions for their collection at the Marineamt; but they will be pigeon holed — nothing more.
> — John Buchan, *The Thirty-Nine Steps*, c. 1915

Author and statesman, John Buchan (1875-1940) was an extraordinarily prolific writer whose works range from a history of World War I to a work on taxation, and include a number of novels in interestingly interrelated genres.[109] Some sixty years later, however, Buchan is perhaps best remembered for his espionage fiction, the success of which overshadowed not only his other literary accomplishments but also the varied and prestigious work he carried out as a British public servant.[110]

Buchan's most celebrated novels are the four espionage stories featuring the prototypical Buchan hero named Richard Hannay: *The Thirty Nine Steps* (1915), *Greenmantle* (1916), *Mr. Standfast* (1919), and *The Three Hostages* (1924). And although his work in the genre is by no means confined to the Hannay "quartet," taken together, they provide perhaps the best examples of, not only Buchan's reliance upon his experience

---

108 McCormick 1977, 44.
109 Buchan enjoyed a successful literary and political career. After World War I ended, he became a director of Reuters, and in 1927 was elected to Parliament. He wrote a novel a year between 1922 and 1936, and produced biographies on James Graham (1928) and Sir Walter Scott (1932), and studies of General Charles Gordon (1934) and Oliver Cromwell (1934). He also held a number of important government posts, serving as Lord High Commissioner of the Church of Scotland (1933-34) and as Governor General of Canada (1935-40).
110 O'Brien 1998, 97.

as an intelligence officer, but also his marked engagement with world geopolitical events as backdrop to his espionage fiction.[111]

John Buchan was born in Scotland and won a bursary to study at Glasgow University. After graduating, he read for the bar and worked as an author and journalist, contributing to *Blackwood's Magazine* and *The Spectator*, before joining the staff of Lord Milner, High Commissioner to South Africa, in 1901. Buchan spent the next two years working on the reconstruction of South Africa following the Boer War before returning to London. From 1903 to 1906, he worked as a barrister and explored a writing career, publishing many short stories and works of nonfiction. In 1907, he was made a director of the publishing firm Thomas Nelson & Son, and in 1910 published *Prester John*, an adventure tale set in South Africa.

During World War I, Buchan was attached as a temporary Lieutenant Colonel to the headquarters staff of the British Army in France and when Lord George became Prime Minister, he was made Director of Information, followed by a period as Director of Intelligence. It was in France that Buchan made the acquaintance of an army officer named Edmund Ironside — soon to command the Allied forces at Archangel to aid Aleksandr Kolchak in fighting the Bolsheviks and later to become Field Marshal Lord Ironside — who was then concerned with intelligence operations in Russia. Buchan later admitted that it was on Ironside that he modeled his fictional character of Richard Hannay.

In *The Thirty-Nine Steps*, Buchan sets the stage for most of his espionage fiction as far as premise and plot are concerned. The primary — and recurring — theme is the character of power, more specifically the uses and abuses of power, with particular emphasis on the international scene. In Buchan's world, the enemy is the one who abuses power, generally by desiring to acquire a monopoly of it, and his violent, subversive, and clandestine maneuvers deliberately disregard the rules of the international power game. For Buchan these rules are the code of honor and due procedure which entitle one nation to the respect of another, and the game is the interplay of competing national interests. Civilization is built on the assumption that the rules can accommodate the game and is sustained on the practical implementation of that

---

111 Ibid.

assumption. Violations of the rules — leading to manipulation of the game — are inevitably expressed in unscrupulous and amoral terms, and the lack of a so-called "institutional responsibility" implied by such violations threatens anarchy and a collapse of the duly constituted, traditional power structure.[112]

Buchan is central to the evolution of the genre for his stories reflect the penetration of enemy espionage networks, depict solitary agents and lonely escapes and, most importantly, expose the thin veneer that stands between civilization and barbarism even in the most elegant drawing room. For his time, Buchan defined the spy story formula and from the appearance of *The Thirty-Nine Steps* until the rise of the disillusioned spy, of the man who has discovered that there is no moral difference between "us" and "them" — that is, until John Le Carré's third book, in 1963, *The Spy Who Came in from the Cold* — the formula remained tied to Buchan. Still, the Buchan formula was certainly not well understood, for most books that appeared under the confident declaration that they were "in the Buchan mold" bore only surface resemblance to that mold, but it was there, a goal to be attained by very few of Buchan's contemporaries.[113]

In *The Thirty-Nine Steps*, Richard Hannay is a wealthy Scot who meets an American journalist named Scudder, who tells of an international assassination plan. Scudder is murdered and Hannay realizes that he himself is the prime suspect. The plot consists essentially of a sustained chase, one of Buchan's main imaginative standbys. Foremost of the novel, Hannay finds himself in a kind of no man's land — suggestive of Cooper's neutral ground — and only Hannay has any inkling of the dastardly plot by enemies (namely the Germans) whose object is to undermine the military capability of the British Navy by stealing its secret plans. But his knowledge leaves him isolated and vulnerable, a citizen pitting his wits against not only enemy powers but also against the police who want Hannay as the prime suspect in Scudder's murder. Hannay escapes to Scotland and, like anybody on the run, is expressly concerned with his own survival. As events unfold, Hannay sees that his own fate and even his identity is inextricably linked with the sur-

112 O'Brien 1998, 101.
113 Winks 1988, xi.

vival of the British fleet and with the even larger issues of national sur-vival that depend on the fleet. In a sense, Hannay is empowered by the urgency of the position in which he finds himself and it is this sense of empowerment that drives him to action.[114, 115]

Hannay possesses but one clue to resolve his predicament: a cryp-tic note found inside the deceased Scudder's notebook. The note reads: "Thirty-nine steps — I counted them — High Tide 10:17 p.m."[116] Hannay correctly deduces that this refers to the location of the anarchists' beach house. Ultimately, Sir Walter Bullivant of the Foreign Office comes to Hannay's assistance. This is a development that not only underlines Hannay's earlier solitariness and the desperation, but it also suggests that access to the corridors of power is the means through which "insti-tutional responsibility" for Hannay's actions is achieved. Without this ratification, Hannay's activities could be considered to be "outside the law" and this would run counter to Buchan's notion of service to King and country. In this context, the entry of Sir Walter — who remains a recurring presence in the Hannay quartet — enables the letter of "na-tional interest" to authenticate the novel's spirit of adventure. Hannay cannot be seen simply as a freelancing, possibly rogue individual, but rather as a tool of the government, drawing out the enemy so that they may be dealt with in the manner proscribed by law.[117]

Greenmantle (1916) has the same basic thriller ingredients and takes Hannay on a mission to the Near East to foil a German-backed *jihad*. Again drawn from actual geopolitical alliances, this plot reflects con-temporary British concerns of Turkey's entry into the war and, in par-ticular, of German attempts to enlist Islamic Turks in support of the German war effort. *Greenmantle* also moves espionage fiction out of its geographic absorption with Britain and the Continent and marginally reawakens the imperial adventure story fostered by Kipling's *Kim*. Mr.

---

114 O'Brien 1998, 101.
115 Buchan's creation, Richard Hannay, became the very model of the "clubland hero" — the denizen of the elite male clubs of London who could turn his good breed-ing, talents, and leisure time to the pursuit of patriotic espionage. As Richard Usborne remarks in his study, *Clubland Heroes* (1953), many secret warriors of Usborne's acquaintance during World War II began the conflict imagining themselves in the mode of Hannay or his companion, Sandy Arbuthnot (Wark 1998, 1203).
116 Buchan 1994, 73.
117 O'Brien 1998, 101-103.

Standfast (1919) follows a similar thread and paints a vivid story of the climax of the war on the western front and Germany's Spring 1918 offensive in which now *Brigadier* Hannay plays a leading role by foiling a German spy plot before returning to his army division where he sees the war to its conclusion.[118]

Buchan may have been less psychologically penetrating than Conrad, but he possessed a stylistic talent well beyond that of Le Queux and Oppenheim. He was also considerably more aware of the "writer's tricks" that the spy novel required, especially its pushing chance and happenstance to the outer limits of probability. In the dedication to *The Thirty-Nine Steps*, to his friend, the publisher Thomas Nelson, Buchan defines the story as "romance where the incidents defy probabilities, and march just inside the borders of the possible."[119] Yet, Buchan's "borders of the possible" are conveyed not through the narrator's insistence but rather through his establishment of a fictional sense of place amid real-life events, characters, and topical concerns.

Buchan's sense of place is perceptive and he makes that sense work for his readers much in the manner of Arthur Conan Doyle. Through the application of landscape, Buchan establishes a sense of moral as well as natural order: the forest, the streams, mountains and lakes are typically identified by the appropriate Scots, or Irish, or Afrikaans word. And by establishing the kind of place in which the action will occur, Buchan subtly tells the reader how to respond to any disturbance within that place while simultaneously remaining within its natural order. Just as Doyle's descriptions of the Devonshire moor in *The Hound of the Baskervilles* establishes far more than simple mood by showing us landscape as a moral environment, so too does Buchan invest the simple movement of a branch in the wind with a sense of menace.[120] As Doyle warned his readers: "Please, please, be frank with me, Miss Stapleton, for ever since I have been here I have been conscious of shadows all round me. Life has become like that great Grimpen Mire, with little green patches everywhere into which one may sink and with no guide to point the track."[121] Buchan made the same point a bit differently on

---

118 Ibid.
119 Buchan 1994, v.
120 Winks 1988, xii.
121 Doyle 1994, 73.

the occasion of his describing the streets of London as landscape in *The Power-House* (1916): "You think that a wall as solid as the earth separates civilization from barbarism. I tell you the division is a thread, a sheet of glass." Thus, in Buchan's world, the environment emerges as a series of dramatic, none-too-subtle contrasts designed to reflect, and indeed indemnify, the vagaries of human nature.[122]

For Buchan, the agent is a moral soldier — again a throwback to Cooper — fortified not only by a mandate from political authority but also by inherited and unquestioned values of decency, tenacity, obedience and devotion to country. His orders are to maintain the world as it is; otherwise, mere anarchy will prevail.[123] To this end, Buchan employed both character and situational factors to provide both a model of form and an inner spirit to the spy novel, giving it through his vision of the life a capacity to express, in terms of contemporary international politics and intrigue, the yearning for a lost world of fullness and heroism.[124] And he succeeded. *The Thirty-Nine Steps* struck exactly the right note and, disregarding its more melodramatic episodes, it had all the right ingredients of the successful spy story: topicality in the midst of war, an exciting chase in which the spy-catcher is pursued by the spy's agents, and a series of cinematic situations amidst splendid background scenery of moor and mountain which made the book a natural for Alfred Hitchcock, who adapted it for the screen in 1935.[125]

Although Buchan himself seemed not to take his spy stories too seriously, they are undoubtedly the expression of, or even the fantasy life of, a man who found himself in the front line of the momentous social and political changes threatened — and to a considerable extent brought into being — by the historical events of the first thirty years of the twentieth century.[126] All of Buchan's espionage novels center themselves on adventure, wherein the protagonist must now save the day instead of seizing it, the latter being his supposedly natural inclination. And not only does Buchan's experience as an insider give a sense of assurance and credibility to the action, but the very fact that much of

---

122 Winks 1988, xii.
123 O'Brien 1998, 109.
124 Cawelti and Rosenberg 1987, 100.
125 McCormick and Fletcher 1990, 40.
126 Liukkonen 2001.

that action takes place in a historically conditioned "here and now" is noteworthy. This is particularly evident in his use of the machinery of modern life — planes in *The Thirty-Nine Steps*, a car chase in *The Island of Sheep*, trains throughout — that also help to give his work additional excitement and a plausible worldliness.[127]

Buchan sought to modernize the spy novel by infiltrating his stories with the actual concerns, dangers, and challenges of his own generation. But, even more importantly, he also struck the first modern note in the evolution of the genre in the degree of doubt and insecurity that over-shadows the mission, a sense of which is tellingly conveyed by the simple device of first-person narration. This same note, greatly amplified and with its dissonance frankly acknowledged, anticipates the imaginative landscapes of such well-known successors as Eric Ambler, Graham Greene, and John Le Carré, whose thrillers may be correctly seen, in part at least, as implicit correctives of Buchan.[128]

127 O'Brien 1998, 109.
128 Ibid.

CHAPTER 4. THE INTERWAR YEARS — TOWARD A DARKER MORALITY

> You see, your businessman desires the end, but dislikes the means. That is why Saridza is necessary. There is always dirty work to be done but whatever it is, Saridza and his kind are there to do it, with large fees in their pockets and the most evasive instructions imaginable.
> — Eric Ambler, *Uncommon Danger*, c. 1937

During the late 1920s and 1930s, there was a distinct shift in both the tone and direction of espionage fiction and the emergence of a new school of spy novelists. The core members of this new school were Somerset Maugham, Eric Ambler and Graham Greene who, collectively, began the progression away from the club land heroes of Buchan's era in favor of more psychologically complex characters. They were also markedly more interested in employing the genre to further probe the uneasy political environment that existed between the two world wars. Maugham, Ambler and Greene sought to course the genre toward a greater reality — and a darker morality — and to generally raise the genre's literary and aesthetic seriousness. Maugham's *Ashenden or The British Agent* (1928) is the earliest example of this new direction thus, in some circles, achieving the distinction of becoming the first realistic spy novel.

W. SOMERSET MAUGHAM ~

> But there will always be espionage and there will always be counter-espionage. Though conditions may have altered, though difficulties may be greater, when war is raging, there will always be secrets which one side jealously guards and which the other will use every means to discover; there will always be men who from malice or for money will betray their kith and kin and there will always be men who, from love of adventure or a sense of duty, will risk a shameful death to secure information valuable to their country.
>
> — W. Somerset Maugham, Preface to *Ashenden or The British Agent*, c1927

One of the most acclaimed and widely read English writers of the twentieth century, William Somerset Maugham (1874-1965) was the son of a wealthy British solicitor assigned to the British Embassy in Paris.[129] However, by the time he was ten, his parents were dead and he was sent to live with an uncle in Whitstable, Kent. After an education at King's School, Canterbury, and Heidelberg University in Germany, Maugham became a medical student at St. Thomas Hospital, London. While training to be a doctor he worked as an obstetric clerk in the slums of Lambeth and used these experiences to help him write his first novel, *Liza of Lambeth* (1897), which prompted Maugham to quit medicine and become a full-time writer.[130]

In the years leading up to World War I, Maugham, became a man-about-town: a successful, urbane and witty satirist of British society.[131] Financially secure, he entertained lavishly and generally enjoyed a Bohemian lifestyle in Paris. But despite Maugham's wealth and fame, during World War I he joined a Red Cross unit in France as a dresser,

---

129 Maugham achieved fame with his play *Lady Frederick* (1907), a comedy about money and marriage. By 1908 Maugham had four plays running simultaneously in London. During the war, Maugham's best-known novel, *Of Human Bondage* (1915), was published. This was followed by another successful book, *The Moon and Sixpence* (1919). Maugham also developed a reputation as a fine short-story writer. One story, "Rain," which appeared in *The Trembling of a Leaf* (1921), was also turned into a successful feature film. Popular plays written by Maugham include *The Circle* (1921), *East of Suez* (1922), *The Constant Wife* (1926) and the anti-war play, *For Services Rendered* (1932). In his later years, Maugham wrote his autobiography, *Summing Up* (1938), and works of fiction such as *The Razor's Edge* (1945), *Catalina* (1948) and *Quartet* (1949).

130 McCormick 1977, 137.

131 Showalter 1997.

ambulance driver and interpreter. Through social connections, he met a British officer, Captain John Wallinger, who had served in India and was currently assigned to the British Secret Intelligence Service. This meeting would prove central to Maugham's understanding of the intelligence service and provide the background for his later writing of *Ashenden or The British Agent,* a collection of short stories, drawn from Maugham's own espionage activities, beginning in Geneva and ending in Petrograd during the Russian Revolution.[132] As Eric Ambler has observed, Ashenden is, "the first fictional work on the subject [the life of the secret agent] by a writer of stature with first-hand knowledge of what he is writing about."[133]

In 1915, Maugham was in London on leave and had dinner with Captain John Arnold Wallinger. Wallinger explained that he had been given the task of restructuring the British espionage force working in Switzerland, where most of the English spies and their foreign agents had been exposed and arrested. He then suggested to Maugham that he serve as a British agent in Switzerland. The idea intrigued Maugham and, with little hesitation, he accepted the assignment. As Maugham later recalled, he was ideally equipped to deal with a number of foreign agents working for the British in that he spoke fluent French and acceptable German, and had the perfect cover: a famous writer living abroad so that he could "write a play in peace and quiet in a neutral country."[134]

Maugham made his way to Lucerne, where his first assignment was to contact an English operative who had a German wife. The man was suspected of being a double agent who was actually working for the Germans. Maugham not only made contact with this agent but also convinced him to go to France, where he was seized and shot as a spy. This episode was later recounted in Maugham's short story *The Traitor,* which is also the story that first introduced his enigmatic fictional

---

132 Maugham gave one clue in his book as to the real identity of Ashenden. The latter's superior officer asked him where he had been living "all these years." "At 36 Chesterfield Street, Mayfair," was Ashenden's reply. This was Maugham's own address before the war (McCormick 1977, 138).

133 McCormick 1977, 138.

134 Maugham 2001.

spy Ashenden, through whom he recounted his own espionage routine while living and working in Geneva. For example:

> Ashenden was on his way back to Geneva. The night was stormy and the wind blew cold from the mountains, but the stodgy little steamer plodded sturdily through the choppy waters of the lake. A scudding rain, just turning into sleet, swept the deck in angry gusts, like a nagging woman who cannot leave a subject alone. Ashenden had been to France in order to write and dispatch a report. A day or two before, about five in the afternoon, an Indian agent of his had come to see him in his rooms; it was only by a lucky chance that he was in, for he had no appointment with him and the agent's instructions were to come to the hotel only in case of urgent importance. He told Ashenden that a Bengali in the German service had recently come from Berlin with a black cane trunk in which were a number of documents interesting to the British Government. At that time the Central Powers were doing their best to foment such an agitation in India as would make it necessary for Great Britain to keep their troops in the country and perhaps send others from France.[135]

Shortly after his Swiss endeavor, Maugham was approached by William Wiseman of British intelligence who wanted Maugham to spy not only for British intelligence but also for the American State Department. Wiseman explained that the war in Russia was going badly and the West feared that, if the Russian war effort collapsed, one of the many political internal forces assailing the Czar's unsteady government would take over and sue for peace with Germany, allowing the Germans to shift forces on the Eastern Front to the Western Front and overwhelm the democracies. As before, Maugham seemed an ideal choice because he spoke Russian, had intelligence experience and was recognized as an author, an ideal cover up for a spy since he could amass information under the pretext of doing research for a book.[136]

Maugham was somewhat taken aback by Wiseman's entreaty. While he was indeed a successful playwright and author, he was certainly no diplomat and understood little of Russia's politics or its chaotic social situation. Nevertheless, as Maugham later wrote: "In 1917 I went to Russia. I was sent to prevent the Bolshevik revolution and to keep Russia in the war."[137] He traveled by ship to Japan and then to

---

135 Maugham 1951, 13.
136 Knightly 1987, 65.
137 Maugham 1951, 9.

Vladivostok to embark on the trans-Siberian railway. In Petrograd, he took a room at the Hotel Europa and set to work, using his renown as a writer to gain access to Russian literary circles. He met the liberal leader, Alexander Kerensky, and several prominent Bolsheviks, and filed voluminous reports to Wiseman, who in turn passed them on to the Americans.

The Bolsheviks came to suspect Maugham soon after his arrival but did nothing to interfere with his work. One reason could have been that since his reports stressed the growing strength of the Bolshevik movement, they were content to let him be. Maugham's views, on the whole, were more accurate than most other reports reaching the West — he gave early warning of Kerensky's declining power, for example — but, perhaps because he was a writer, he was overly optimistic about the influence of propaganda and somewhat naive in its application. This naiveté was clearly demonstrated by one of Maugham's suggestions for countering the Bolsheviks and keeping the Russians fighting. He suggested that the Americans should make newsreels showing the life of the working classes in America, pictures of Washington and New York, and some pictures of German militarism and what it meant.[138] But, whatever his shortcomings as a propagandist, the November Revolution soon put an end to Maugham's spying. Kerensky, dressed as a woman, had escaped across the Finnish border, and Maugham felt that he himself was now a marked man and that his work with Kerensky had been for nothing. He was also suffering the effects of tuberculosis and was depressed and shocked by the sudden change in events. He slipped out of Russia and returned to Britain.[139]

Maugham's service as a secret agent remained a distinctive memory for him, one that elevated his sense of excitement and, to some extent, supported the notion that he had made some measure of contribution to the greater Western cause. While trying to save Kerensky's government — naive as he and the British government were at that time in dealing with the Bolsheviks — he nonetheless believed that his espionage activities had been important and, moreover, that he was now a

---

138 Knightly 1987, 65.
139 Perhaps the most comprehensive examination of Maugham's sojourn in Russia can be found in R.J. Jeffery-Jones' *American Espionage*, New York: The Free Press, 1977.

charter member of some small, secret fraternity. This feeling was clearly expressed in a 1917 letter to a friend: "It seems incredible that one of these days we shall all settle down again to normal existence and read the fat, peaceful *Times* every morning and eat porridge for breakfast and marmalade. But, my dear, we shall be broken relics of a dead era, on the shelf all dusty and musty."[140]

Still, while *Ashenden or The British Agent* was the articulated result of Maugham's espionage experience, it also contrasted markedly with the heroics, high life and exaggerated stereotypes of Oppenheim, Le Queux and Buchan. *Ashenden* offered the general public its first exposure to what espionage was really like — not romantic melodrama, but long periods of boredom, fear, human weakness, callousness and deceit.[141]

In fact, *Ashenden or The British Agent* is a collection of linked short stories, beginning in Geneva and ending in Petrograd during the revolution. The agent, Ashenden, who is the principal character in all of the stories, is in many ways a self-portrait of Maugham himself and was perhaps the first of the antiheroes, not a brilliant performer of courageous deeds but a rather orderly, anxious man who worried about missing trains and had an attack of nerves when a fellow agent was about to murder a Greek spy.[142] And it is precisely this type of antiheroic vision — sketched against the mundane reality of the spy's existence — that made Maugham's work a model for later writers.[143] As Maugham himself says of Ashenden's more commonplace activities:

> Ashenden's official existence was as orderly and monotonous as a city clerk's. He saw his spies at stated intervals and paid them their wages; when he could get hold of a new one he engaged him, gave him his instructions and sent him off to Germany; he waited for the information that came through and dispatched it; he went into France once a week to confer with his colleague over the frontier and to receive his orders from London; he visited the

---

140 Maugham 2001.

141 McCormick and Fletcher 1990, 183.

142 In 1936, film director Alfred Hitchcock adapted Maugham's novel for the screen in *The Secret Agent* with John Gielgud cast as the Ashenden character. Hitchcock had convinced Gielgud to play the lead in *The Secret Agent* by describing Ashenden as a modern day Hamlet who could not resolve to do his duty. But many, including Gielgud himself, ended up disliking the Ashenden character, feeling that he was an enigma, and considerably more loathsome than the film's villain.

143 Cawelti and Rosenberg 1987, 45.

marketplace on market-day to get any messages the old butter-woman had brought him from the other side of the lake; he kept his eyes and ears open; and he wrote long reports which he was convinced no one read till having inadvertently slipped a jest into one of them he received a sharp rebuke for his levity.[144]

Maugham also — through the fictional Ashenden — for the first time in espionage fiction, provided remarkable insight into the considerations of an agent's relationship with his country's embassy. The ambassadors of Great Britain and the United States had been directed to afford him such facilities as were at their command, but Ashenden had been told privately to keep to himself; he was not to make difficulties for the official representatives of the two powers by divulging information to them that it might be inconvenient for them to know. On the contrary, it might be necessary for Ashenden to give clandestine support to a party that was at odds with the ambassadors or, conversely, undermine a party with whom relations with the United States and Great Britain were quite cordial. In either case, Maugham noted, "It was just as well that Ashenden should keep his own counsel. The exalted personages did not wish the ambassadors to suffer the affront of discovering that an obscure agent had been sent to work at cross-purposes with them." On the other hand, Maugham also notes that "...it was thought to be just as well to have a representative in the opposite camp, who, in the event of a sudden upheaval, would be at hand with adequate funds and hold the confidence of the new leaders of the country."[145]

Maugham then, for the first time in a spy novel, offers his observations of an Ambassador's opinion of espionage activities and, in particular, of its agents:

> Ambassadors are sticklers for their dignity and they have a keen nose to scent any encroachment on their authority. When Ashenden on his arrival at X paid an official call on Sir Herbert Witherspoon, the British ambassador, he was received with a politeness to which no exception could be taken, but with a frigidity that would have sent a little shiver down the spine of a polar bear. Sir Herbert was a diplomat de carrière and he cultivated the manner of his profession to a degree that filled the observer

---

144 Maugham 1951, 70.
145 Ibid., 128.

with admiration. He did not ask Ashenden anything about his mission because he knew that Ashenden would reply evasively, but he allowed him to see that it [the mission] was a perfectly foolish one. He talked with acidulous tolerance of the exalted personages who had sent Ashenden to X. He told Ashenden that he had instructions to meet any demands for help that he made and stated that if Ashenden at any time desired to see him he had only to say so.[146]

While Maugham's emphasis on the more practical and bureaucratic aspects of espionage have played a fundamental role in the evolution of spy novel, it was his mood of cynicism and his development of the antiheroic protagonist that was most strongly echoed in the work of his immediate successors, Eric Ambler and Graham Greene. Beginning with Greene's *Orient Express* in the early 1930s and continuing with such superb spy adventures as *This Gun for Hire*, *The Ministry of Fear*, and *The Confidential Agent*, and Ambler's *The Mask of Dimitrios*, *Epitaph for a Spy*, and *Journey into Fear*, Ambler and Greene created a new version of the espionage genre that dominated the literature until the 1950s.[147]

For his part, Maugham was well aware of *Ashenden*'s influence on the genre, for he later observed: "There is a school of novelists that looks upon this as the proper model for [spy] fiction. If life, they say, is arbitrary and disconnected, why fiction should be so too; for fiction should imitate life. In life things happen at random, and that is how they should happen in a story; they do not lead to a climax, which is an outrage to probability, they just go on."[148]

When contrasted against the world events of Maugham's era, *Ashenden* offers a notable blending of fact and fiction and remarkable insight into the secret world of intelligence activities as witnessed through the eyes of an actual agent. *Ashenden* was Maugham's sole espionage novel; perhaps after its publication and widespread critical acceptance, he realized that any other ventures into spy fiction would have been anticlimactic, for he was a wise enough writer to realize he had set a new standard in the evolution of the spy novel and, presumably, he felt his work there was finished.[149]

---

146 Ibid., 129.
147 Cawelti and Rosenberg 1987, 46.
148 Maugham 1951, 7.
149 McCormick and Fletcher 1990, 184.

ERIC AMBLER ~

> But to me the most important thing to know about an assas-
> sination is not who fired a shot — but who paid for the bullet.
> — Eric Ambler, *The Mask of Dimitrios*, c. 1939

Eric Ambler (1909-1998) was one of the foremost architects of espionage fiction as it exists today. Like Maugham — and Ambler's contemporary Graham Greene — Ambler also sought to transform the genre from the verbal banality and minimal characterizations of Le Queux and Oppenheim to a more morally ambiguous world of decep-tion and danger. Ambler also coursed the genre in another measurably different direction by moving away from the more conservative, pro-British "King and Crown" intrigues to explore other political venues. As Ambler himself later said, "I looked around for something I could change and decided it was the thriller-espionage story. I decided to turn that upside down and make the heroes left wing and popular front figures."[150] To this end he was extraordinarily successful. Between the years 1936 and 1940 Ambler wrote six classic spy novels: *The Dark Frontier* (1936), *Uncommon Danger* (1937), *Epitaph for a Spy* (1938), *Cause for Alarm* (1938), *The Mask of Dimitrios* (1939), and *Journey Into Fear* (1940).

Eric Ambler embraced the spy novel at a critical juncture. By 1936, Childers, Chesterton, Conrad and Le Queux were dead; Oppenheim had grown excessively tedious and largely unreadable; Buchan was serving as the Governor-General of Canada and had largely forsaken the genre; and Maugham had left England amid a sex scandal and moved to France where he was writing short stories and plays. Into this void stepped Amber, who took the spy story by its patrician neck, plucked the monocle from its eye, and pulled it down into the world of the com-mon man, far away from the world diplomatic aristocrats.[151] One critic, when evaluating Ambler's contribution to the genre, observes: "At last Ambler came; and from his *Uncommon Danger* (1937) we may date the transfiguration of the spy story. Ambler showed that human character-ization, good prose, political intelligence, and above all a meticulously

---

150 Ambler 1998, 133.
151 Sandoe 1946, 260.

detailed realism, far from getting in the way of intricate spy adventures, can strengthen them and raise them to a new plane."[152]

Eric Ambler was born in London where he attended London University. After college, he briefly worked in advertising, before moving to Paris where he dedicated himself to writing. Since Buchan, the British spy novel had become extremely formulaic and increasingly anti-Semitic, jingoistic and xenophobic: the very traits that Ambler — by the mid-1930s — had decided were hopelessly anachronistic.[153] But, instead of lamenting the gloomy state of the genre, he saw in it considerable potential for exploring more serious issues, particularly the numerous geopolitical crises in Europe drawn the rise of Fascism in Italy and Nazism in Germany.

Like many young intellectuals during the interwar years, Ambler was attracted by socialist ideas and supported the Popular Front, although he never became a Communist. During the 1930s he spent as much time as possible traveling in Europe and was fully aware of the nature of totalitarian regimes as well as the threat they posed to peace. And this is seemingly what attracted Ambler to espionage rather than the detective story. In the spy novel, he found the ability to encompass international action and topical themes, such as the economic conflict between capitalism and socialism, and the political battles between the Right and the Left. It could, therefore, transcend contemporary closed-world, middle class biases and engage the major political issues of the day.[154] Too, as a more practical matter, there was also no shortage of potential plots. Arms dealers and industrialists were widely credited in the early 1930s with pursuing profits at the expense of peace and thereby spawning World War I. This image was further solidified upon the onset of the Depression that gave further credence to the notion of the capitalist and industrialist as forces not of harmony and stability but of menace, with their collective greed and moral ambiguity acknowledged as a clear and present danger to world order.[155]

Against this backdrop, Ambler sought to cast his new spy protagonist as one who begins as an innocent and finds himself slowly trapped

---

152 Boucher 1946, 245.
153 Lewis 1998, 14.
154 Ibid.
155 Stafford 1998, 133.

and sometimes crushed by the forces of politics, espionage and the incomprehensibility of life beyond the frontiers of Britain, especially life in the strife-ridden Balkans. Ambler's opinion on the industrialist arms dealers' "merchants of death" conspiracy is clearly reflected in his first novel, *The Dark Frontier*, when one of the characters, Professor Bairstow, guilelessly states: "It looked as if there would always be wars....What else could you expect from a balance of power adjusted in terms of land, of arms, of man-power and of materials: in terms, in other words, of money?...Wars were made by those who had the power to upset the balance, to tamper with international money and money's worth."[156]

While *Dark Frontier* was far from being one of Ambler's more memorable books, it marked a revolutionary, disillusioned, and even cynical approach to the espionage story. Further, his interpretation of the world situation, however dark, was reflective of the circa 1930s' popular opinion wherein most thinking people realized the hollowness of the politicians' pretence that World War I was "the war to end all wars." Aggressive forces were on the march all over Europe and in the Balkans, democracy was being spelt out as a dirty word, and the private manufacture of arms was aiding the enemies of democracy more than the countries that actually produced the weapons.

Still, Ambler struck a note of neutralism in his spy novels, sharply and astringently enlightening the reader that, in the pursuit of espionage, one side was really as bad as the other and that spies and spy-catchers were not only principally un-heroic but very often of minor significance and unpleasant mien.[157] Thus, in Ambler's vision, agents and spies were not splendid patriots but hired killers; and his stories of espionage sought to reveal certain truths of the matter, thus extinguishing any lingering romantic notions as promoted by Buchan, Oppenheim, and his other predecessors.

In Ambler's second novel, *Uncommon Danger*, the central character, Nicholas Kenton, is an archetypal antihero rather than the conventional ultra-patriotic hero of earlier thrillers. A cosmopolitan journalist, Kenton emerges as the model for what will become, in subsequent novels, the typical Ambler protagonist: an ordinary, unexceptional person

---

156 Ambler 1977, 22.
157 McCormick 1977, 22.

who, by virtue of being in the wrong place at the wrong time, is suddenly involved in a network of political and criminal duplicity of which he was previously unaware.

In *Uncommon Danger*, Ambler also seeks to refine his sense of sinister realism. And while it can be argued that the plot structure of *Uncommon Danger* in some respects resembles that of Buchan's *The Thirty-Nine Steps*, critics immediately saw that Ambler's approach was refreshingly new and different, with the plot firmly embedded in the real-life European political triad that had emerged battleground of the 1930s: socialism against capitalism, Marxism against fascism, and democracy against totalitarianism. Indeed, the Soviet military secrets around which the novel is based relate specifically to an actual source of European tension, the oil-producing region of Romania which was claimed by the Soviet Union.[158] He then gives added credibility to his fictional conspiracy involving governments and big business by including references to contemporary politicians and organizations.[159]

Another aspect of Ambler's subversion of the standard spy novel is the reversal of its characteristic ideological stance. His satire of big business and monopoly capitalism, represented by the multinational Pan-Eurasian Petroleum Company, as well as his sympathetic treatment of a brother-and-sister pair of Soviet agents, Andreas and Tamara Zaleshoff, make this a left-wing novel, which was a startling innovation at the time. But in broadly endorsing socialist values, Ambler concurrently attacks British insularity for its refusal to acknowledge the political degeneration of continental Europe. With this viewpoint, Ambler brought an unexpected sophistication to the genre and, both stylistically and formalistically, his early novels are much subtler than the standard British spy novels of the time, offering in the late 1930s a unique, if pessimistic view, of the world situation, principally in their portrayal of Nazism from a non-British, more "third person" point of view. This is particularly evident in *Epitaph for a Spy* and *Cause for Alarm*.[160]

---

158 Bessarabia is a region in Eastern Europe that was historically part of Romania-Moldova until 1812, when Russia seized it after defeating the Ottoman Empire. It roughly coincides with today's so-called of Republic of Moldova.
159 Lewis 1998, 15.
160 Ibid.

Structurally, *Epitaph for a Spy* is closer to the English detective novel than to the fast-moving thriller, but Ambler handles the form in his own unique way so that his political concerns are never far from the surface. The story is set in the relatively closed world of a hotel in the south of France. Yet, despite its quiet hotel setting, *Epitaph for a Spy* effectively reaches out to embrace the political happenings in Europe at the time. Ambler peoples the hotel with a varied and cosmopolitan cadre, including Nazi agents and anti-Nazi Marxists, so that the hotel can thus be seen as a microcosm of the many tensions tearing Europe apart at the end of the 1930s. Knowing that among the twelve people in the hotel is a spy gathering information about French naval secrets, the police pressure one of these, the first-person narrator Vadassy, to help them from the inside. Like Ambler's customary protagonists, the ethnically Hungarian Vadassy is an ordinary person who has the misfortune to find himself in the middle of something sinister through no fault of his own. Yet, as a stateless person without any family — and very much a victim of the calamities and redrawn boundaries in Eastern Europe after World War I — Vadassy emerges as the consummate Ambler outsider and loner. The French police exploit Vadassy's vulnerability to make him cooperate, but Vadassy's efforts at detection prove to be extremely clumsy. As it comes to pass, the police actually discovered the identity of the spy at the hotel early in their investigation, and Vadassy's role as amateur detective is a subterfuge by the French police to help them identify an entire Italian spy ring rather than a solitary operative.[161]

In *Epitaph for a Spy*, Ambler creates a totally unexpected blend of the spy novel and the classical detective story that turns out to be different from either one. Yet he plays with both formulas in such a way as to produce a political novel of considerable topicality and, published a year before World War II began, the novel is full of portents of conflict as European civilization teetered on the edge of war.[162] As Ambler noted in an afterword to the novel: "I wrote *Epitaph for a Spy* in 1937, and it was a mild attempt at realism. The central character is a stateless

---

161 Ibid., 16.
162 Ibid.

person, there are no professional devils, and the only Britisher in the story is anything but stalwart. I still like bits of it."[163]

With *Cause for Alarm* Ambler returned to the pattern of the alternative thriller he had developed in *Uncommon Danger*, but with more sophistication and subtlety. The main setting is Mussolini's Italy rather than central or eastern Europe, and includes a chapter in the British edition — it was excised in the first American edition — that details an account of how a brilliant Italian scientist was gradually driven insane by his treatment under the Fascists. The narrative of pursuit and escape inevitably slows down for such discursive treatment of the history of Italian Fascism, but it does provide the novel with more historical breadth and political depth than it would have had otherwise.

Whereas the plots of Ambler's earlier novels hinge on the familiar device of a quest for secret documents, that of *Cause for Alarm* involves an ingenious intelligence ploy by the Soviet agent Andreas Zaleshoff to plant information designed to cause a rift between his ideological enemies: Hitler's Germany and Mussolini's Italy. Any damage to their Berlin-Rome Axis would postpone, if only temporarily, the risk of war. Just as Kenton cooperates with Zaleshoff in *Uncommon Danger*, a young English engineer, Marlow, becomes Zaleshoff's associate in *Cause for Alarm*, and most of the novel is told from Marlow's point of view. Like Kenton, Marlow is the antitype of the conventional thriller hero, but is more naive and insular in his liberalism. The opportunity to run his small company's Milan office proves to be Marlow's baptism by fire, bringing him face to face with the political nightmares of contemporary Europe and the moral incongruities of serving commercial interests by cooperating with tyrannical regimes.[164]

On one side is General Vagas, a senior Nazi spy who offers Marlow bribes to provide secret information about the Italian armaments industry. On the other is Zaleshoff with his Marxist analysis of the "gospel of King Profit" and his determination to do what he can to preserve European peace by undermining, at least to some extent, the Berlin-Rome Axis. Marlow sides with Zaleshoff and is able to feed Vagas intelligence about Italy's secret military airfields, information being

---

163 Ambler 1938.
164 Lewis 1998, 17.

deliberately concealed from Germany. While Zaleshoff and Marlow eventually do achieve their aim, their success is much more muted than Zaleshoff's victory at the end of *Uncommon Danger*. The novel ends in midair with "But..." Yet the qualified optimism of the epilogue proved illusory for, within a year, Europe was again at war.[165]

Ambler next wrote *The Mask of Dimitrios* which, for many readers, remains his best spy novel, emerging not only as an espionage story but as an imaginative history of the decisive years between the World War I and the rise of Hitler, when Britain, France, the United States and the other powers position themselves for influence and power while the situation in Eastern Europe, Russia, the Balkans, the Mediterranean and the Middle and Far East deteriorated, making World War II all but inevitable.

In *The Mask of Dimitrios* Ambler returns his attention to the Balkans. Charles Latimer, a British academic with a sideline in writing detective fiction, finds himself on holiday in Turkey, where he is socially cornered by a high-ranking member of the Turkish police. This policeman, Colonel Haki, is a fan of detective fiction and very much wants to give Latimer the plot for his next book. Latimer has had many such helpful sessions with fans before and is trying to find a graceful exit when Colonel Haki, after being momentarily distracted by real police business, looks at Latimer speculatively and asks, "I wonder if you are interested in real murderers, Mr. Latimer?"[166]

Latimer rises to the occasion and begins to learn the story of Dimitrios Makropolous, a criminal and spy whose body had recently ended up in police custody after being pulled out of the Bosphorus by a fisherman. Dimitrios' background is sketchy, but he had been implicated in at least one murder for hire, might have worked as a spy for France, had trafficked in narcotics, and had somehow been involved in a political assassination. Certain parts of his past travels are well known, while several years of his background are entirely blank. Stung in part by Colonel Haki's intimation that although he writes of murderers he knows nothing about them, Latimer somewhat impulsively embarks upon "an experiment in detection." He tries to retrace Dimitrios' prog-

---

165 Ibid.
166 Ambler 1996, 10.

ress, at first by trying to visit all the countries where he had made an impact. Along the way Latimer cannot avoid meeting some of Dimitrios' former associates and the experiment in detection becomes less and less academic.[167]

The principal innovation in *The Mask of Dimitrios* is the slow manner in which Ambler reveals pieces of Dimitrios' story, even though the need for the details of that story becomes more and more urgent for Latimer. Along the way, the reader sees much that is surprising about 1930s Europe: a white-slavery racket, the heroin trade, and the tricks of the espionage market for military secrets. The resulting double-layer plot is complicated and touches on elements of post-World War I history that have largely been lost to casual modern readers.

But the novel also brings a subtle Marxist viewpoint into play. Dimitrios is presented not merely as a morally degenerate individual but also as the symptom of a diseased society rooted in capitalist exploitation, one that prioritizes money at the expense of moral and spiritual values. Despite the reference to Hitler's autobiographical *Mein Kampf* in the novel, Ambler nowhere draws parallels between Dimitrios and Hitler; but, upon closer inspection, these may have been at the back of his mind. Like Hitler, Dimitrios was born in 1889, began to attract attention in the early 1920s, was involved in a political coup in 1923, achieved outward respectability and a position of power in the early 1930s, and interfered in the affairs of other countries in the late 1930s.[168] And this, it seems, appears to be something considerably more than coincidence, for in September 1939 Adolf Hitler precipitated World War II.

The outbreak of hostilities soon brought Ambler's career as a novelist to a standstill, but before it did so, he quickly wrote the sixth and last book of his first phase, *Journey into Fear*, which directly braced the German threat of the period. Although less ambitious than *The Mask of Dimitrios*, it breaks new ground in one important respect: it is the most psychological of his early spy novels. In it Ambler undertakes a study in depth of one of his typical antiheroes, Graham, a scientist who initially seems an embodiment of English insularity: conventional, unimaginative, and politically unaware. A leading expert in the arms industry,

---

167 Kelly 1998, 86-89.
168 Lewis 1998, 18.

Graham is capable of making a significant contribution to the war effort against Germany because of his knowledge of Turkey's secret military plans. However, due to this knowledge, Graham finds himself targeted by a Nazi assassination squad while on a mission to Turkey. Like Kenton and Marlow, Graham is an English innocent abroad who unexpectedly finds himself at the center of a malevolent plot. [169]

Primarily set on a ship in the Mediterranean with a small number of passengers, *Journey into Fear* is a closed-world narrative not unlike the hotel-based *Epitaph for a Spy* and involves a similar range of cosmopolitan characters. Graham, having survived one attempt on his life in Turkey, is soon aware that his would-be assassin is also on board the ship and has little difficulty identifying him. While building the requisite tension and suspense, Ambler also keeps the political dimension in the foreground through Graham's introspection and psychological analysis. Finding himself in the psychological equivalent of a death cell, Graham is forced to reassess his entire outlook on life, including politics, and experiences a kind of enlightenment. The boat journey becomes a journey of self-discovery, with fear being the necessary stimulus. Coming to terms with reality, Graham finds within himself the strength to resist what seems inevitable — his murder — and even finds the determination to fight back. In this way he personifies Britain's need to take on the Nazi threat. Whereas Kenton and Marlow experienced a change of heart and mind through the influence of others and succeed by joining forces with Zaleshoff, Graham has to rely entirely on his own resources. Here, in the only novel Ambler wrote during wartime, his characteristic antihero, alone and under intense pressure, becomes a heroic, even patriotic emblem of Britain's resistance to Nazism. Whatever the odds against him, Graham chooses not only to battle it out rather than submit fatalistically, but also, if possible, to win. [170]

Ambler's novels also witnessed the rise of a new class of readers. As to why this occurred, it seems that the interest in and the power of his novels arose not only from the figurations of fascism and capitalism but also in the figuration of a new class, a new character, in the popular imagination: a class of professionals and managers, engineers

---

169 Ibid.
170 Ibid., 19.

and technicians. The people in this class in many ways are the hired guns of capitalism; nevertheless they do work for a wage — if thinly disguised as a salary — and their only real capital lies in the certifications of university training. And it was this class of society that increasingly became the readership of Ambler's serious and literate espionage stories.[171]

Journey into Fear also holds another distinction. It appears to signal a shift in Ambler's political position following the outbreak of war. Ambler later admitted that he was still surprised that he so readily decided that the lead character and object of the reader's sympathy and concern in *Journey into Fear* should be an arms salesman. "This would have been almost unthinkable in the earlier prewar novels, in three of which the company Graham works for, Cator and Bliss, represents the worst side of capitalism — heartless, money-grubbing, and warmongering."[172]

While completing *Journey into Fear* Ambler correctly presumed that, when faced with the scenario of World War II, he would almost certainly not be able to finish another novel if he began it. And while he did indeed continue writing after the cessation of hostilities, Ambler's most significant contributions to the evolution of espionage fiction rest in the publication of his prewar novels. Accordingly, we perhaps owe more to Eric Ambler than to any other espionage novelist because he rescued the spy novel from the kind of slough into which the detective novel had fallen. At a time when most spy writers were congenital Tories he applied his enlightened intelligence to the political background of espionage. And, without Ambler, it seems highly unlikely that either Le Carré or Deighton would have emerged.[173]

As indicated in an interview conducted some three years before his death, Ambler was not only aware of the extent to which world political affairs held sway over the genre but also the importance of maintaining some measure of neutralism while writing an espionage novel:

> Early in my life and books, I was a little to the left. I voted Labour in 1945, but that was the extent of my political involvement. What I believe in is political and social justice. I'm of the same generation as [Graham] Greene. While he was hostile to

---

171 Denning 1987, 78-79.
172 Ambler 1965, iv.
173 Atkins 1984, 247.

America, he was never rude about it. I never put the Cold War
in any of my books. Never took sides during the Cold War, not
that I was a closet Communist. I always found the Cold War
distasteful. For my wartime generation, it meant taking the best
years of your life and turning them around. After the war, nobody
wanted to return to prewar conditions. They had dreams of an
improved way of life. Unfortunately, the Cold War did not help
those dreams.[174]

GRAHAM GREENE ~

It really pays to murder, and when a thing pays, it becomes
respectable. Your old-fashioned murderer killed from fear, from
hate — or even from love, very seldom for substantial profit. None
of these reasons is quite — respectable. But to murder for position — that's different, because when you've gained the position,
nobody has a right to criticize the means. Nobody will refuse to
meet you if the position's high enough. Think of how many of
your statesmen have shaken hands with Hitler.
— Graham Greene, *Ministry of Fear*, 1943

Like Somerset Maugham, Graham Greene (1904-1991) is, for want
of a better term, a "mainline" writer who turned his hand to espionage
fiction and did so successfully. Greene's influence has been profound
and his unsentimental approach to some of the less attractive aspects of
modern life, such as failure, has had considerable and lasting appeal for
later generations of more serious spy novelists.[175] Additionally — and
again similar to Maugham — Greene benefited from real life experience
in the intelligence service.[176]

Graham Greene was one of the most prolific writers of the twentieth century and earned both popular and critical acclaim in a literary
career that ran from the mid-1920s to his death in 1991. By the late 1930s,

---

174 Ambler 1995.

175 In August 1941, Greene joined the British Secret Intelligence Service and was
assigned to Freetown, Sierra Leone, in December. The job was by and large
boring, and Greene livened it up by coming up with some innovative plans to
recruit spies: one proposed a traveling brothel and another involved tricking
a Left Wing official into escaping from Freetown prison with British agents,
letting him cross over into Vichy Territory, and then luring him back to blackmail him into becoming a double agent. Unfortunately he did not obtain ap-
proval for these schemes. In early 1943, Greene returned to London, where he
was reassigned to Counter-Intelligence (Section V) in Portugal, and reported
to, and became friends with, Kim Philby, who was later to be identified as a
Soviet double agent.

176 Atkins 1984, 191.

he was seen as one of the finest English novelists of his generation, and by the end of the 1940s he had acquired an international reputation. When serious critical attention began to be paid to his work in the 1950s, it focused primarily on his novels such as *Brighton Rock* (1938), *The Power and the Glory* (1940), *The Heart of the Matter* (1948), and *The End of the Affair* (1951). Yet long before this Greene had proved himself a success-ful and increasingly popular writer with a number of espionage fictions including *Stamboul Train* (1932), *It's a Battlefield* (1934), *England Made Me* (1935), *A Gun for Sale* (1936), *The Confidential Agent* (1939), and *The Min-istry of Fear* (1943) that, to varying degrees, transformed the espionage genre as it was passed down from Erskine Childers, John Buchan, and the others.[177] Like his contemporaries Maugham and Ambler, Greene sought to elevate the spy novel as medium for serious fiction, a fact that emerges as one of his greatest technical achievement.[178]

Graham Greene was born in 1904 and studied at the Berkhamstead School and Oxford. He wrote quite regularly in student magazines and was an editor of *The Oxford Outlook*. After graduation, he worked briefly for the *Nottingham Journal* before moving to London as the Sub Editor for *The Times*.[179] Greene's attention to the espionage genre began with a con-tradictory project: it combined his dissatisfaction with earlier thrillers with a faith in the possibilities, and indeed the peculiar relevance, of espionage fiction. This perspective, and the sense that the thrillers of Buchan and Oppenheim — the pulp espionage novels of the 1920s — were no longer convincing, brought him to the conclusion that the spy novel had a certain privileged relation to the modern world.[180] "An early hero of mine was John Buchan," Greene wrote. "But when I reopened his books I found I could no longer get the same pleasure from the ad-ventures of Richard Hannay. More than the dialogue and the situation had dated: the moral climate was no longer that of my boyhood. Patrio-tism had lost its appeal, even for a schoolboy, at Passchendaele...while it was difficult, during the years of the Depression, to believe in the

---

177 *Stamboul Train* and *A Gun for Sale* were both published in the United States as, re-spectively, *The Orient Express* and *This Gun for Hire*. Both novels were subsequently adapted for the screen.
178 Diemert 1998, 459; Sharrock 1984, 12.
179 McCormick and Fletcher 1990, 114.
180 Denning 1987, 61.

high purposes of the City of London or of the British Constitution.[181] The hunger marchers seemed more real than the politicians. It was no longer a Buchan world. The hunted man of *This Gun for Hire*, which I now began to write, was Raven, not Hannay: a man out to revenge himself for all the dirty tricks of life, not to save his country."[182]

Accordingly, Greene approaches the genre as an attempt to resolve this contradiction, this sense that the topical themes and styles of earlier writers had become a pointless exercise and, again like Maugham and Ambler, he too finds the solution to be something akin to "realism" — but it is a progressive realism that functions with different meanings and in different ways. Greene, for example, connotes a certain view of reality where violence and brutality are fundamental, where the decorums of "civilized" behavior are but a thin veil over naked power relations where nations and empires are less the expression of a civilizing mission than the mask for exploitation, and where the ethic of sportsmanship and the game is at best an anachronism or, at worst, a mystification.[183]

A second aspect of Greene's fiction is its "seriousness." It manifests itself primarily as a concern for moral dilemmas — for the ambiguities and uncertainties of ethical behavior — and for the questions of loyalty and betrayal. Unlike earlier spy novels, with their straightforward moral schema that designated hero and villain as good and evil and authorized the actions of the hero by the transcendent value of the nation and his sporting observance of the rules of the game, Greene-era "serious" fiction takes as its subject the uncertainty of the authority for the protagonist's actions, the lack of a clear-cut "good," and the ensuing issues of innocence and experience, of identity and point of view.[184] The scenario in Greene's *A Gun For Sale* (1936) is an example of this pattern. James Raven is a hired killer with a harelip, and his profession and his deformity combine to give him a passion for privacy. But, too, the harelip emerges as vivid sign of Greene's compassion for Raven. The harelip,

---

181 Greene's mention of Passchendaele refers to the World War I battle at Passchendaele, Belgium. Officially known as the Battles of Ypres (1917), it witnessed the first German deployment of mustard gas and nearly 600,000 lives were lost in the two and a half month engagement.

182 Greene 1980, 54.

183 Denning 1987, 62.

184 Ibid 63.

by excluding him from society, leads him to a life of crime and sin, and he flashes the harelip angrily on people to punish them for excluding him. But besides expressing his social defiance and inner pain, the harelip also handicaps him as a criminal, and the society that has driven him out does not even let him live comfortably outside its pale. Rather, it brings out his worst traits by encouraging him to cultivate technical cunning and murderousness out of a need to stay alive.[185]

While Greene probed the genre with *A Gun For Sale*, it was shortly prior to World War II before he actually introduced elements of the espionage story into his work. This occurred most notably in *The Confidential Agent* (1939) in which he introduced "D," the agent of an imaginary Latin government bearing a distinct resemblance to that of the beleaguered Spanish Republican government of that era. Everything is seen through the eyes of the confidential agent — himself already tortured by world events — and lived through in a few days of concentrated experiences. As sketched by Greene, the agent functions in a sort of conscious nightmare. He carries the infection of war with him, feeling not only war's destruction but also war's ubiquitous and self-perpetuating suspicion. Yet he is by nature and habit a peaceful man, coming to a peaceful country on an errand which for all its wartime importance was peaceful in itself. His country had been fighting a civil war for two years and he, a professor of romance languages and a famous scholar, had been sent to England to buy coal. The novel's immediate suggestiveness lies, of course, in the fact that the nightmare is also a prophecy: this is modern war, replete with anarchy and destruction, treachery, and ever-widening circles of distrust. But Greene's message implies that the violence and evil and pity are not solely symptoms of war; for human life always carries its seeds of anarchy, brutality, fear and tragic waste, and that man must find his own courage and hope, even through war, if and as he can.[186]

Greene followed *The Confidential Agent* with the publication of *Ministry of Fear* in 1943. Written during the early years of World War II, this was his final work prior to the end of hostilities. *Ministry of Fear* carries a Nazi villain theme and is the story of Arthur Rowe surviving, but not

---

185 Wolfe 1972, 55.
186 Woods 1939.

truly living, in the shadow of what was once his life. Set against the backdrop of London during the Blitz, Rowe finds himself hunted by espionage agents — a German fifth column operating in Britain — after he unwittingly unravels a secret code. Rowe is soon enmeshed in a subterranean chase, pursued by hidden Nazis, clandestine police, and a lovely woman who might or might not be a spy for the Germans. As for Rowe, his persona is nothing less than Greene's illustration of the schizophrenia that was corroding the world at the time. Probably no one else would have chosen Rowe as a protagonist. When he ghosts into the novel, he is dank with malaise, a tall, stooping, lean man with black hair and a sharp narrow face. As Greene describes, his "clothes were good, but gave the impression of being uncared for: you would have said a bachelor if it had not been for an indefinable married look." And yet, when the story ends, he has developed a strange courage.[187]

After World War II, Greene continued to write and produced a sizeable body of critically acclaimed work, including three books relative to the genre of espionage fiction: *The Quiet American* (1955), a political novel about the war in Indochina, employing its characters less as individuals than as representatives of their nations or political factions; *Our Man in Havana* (1958), a humorous examination of a Havana branch manager of an English vacuum-cleaner firm recruited by British intelligence; and *The Human Factor* (1978), a complex story involving a British Secret Service agent working in London who is also a Russian double agent. Collectively, Greene's influence on the evolution of espionage fiction is considerable, particularly with regard to his perception of the human psyche and the motivational influences of good and evil or, in some cases, his merchandising of evil at the expense of good. As Greene himself commented:

> I'm interested in human beings. They aren't saints and they aren't evil men as a rule. I should have thought that only in one book had I tried to write about a wholly unpleasant character, and then at the end one put in a doubt whether even he was as theologically damned as he seemed. Some people would say that there was a sense of morality inculcated into man at the beginning, that conscience is inherited in most people. I don't think I've ever met anybody who was without a conscience. Environment would have an effect, a religious belief would have an effect.

187 DuBois 1943.

> Happiness and misery have their effect, too. Unhappiness isn't always purgative; it can destroy a man. And happiness isn't always selfish; it can make a man less selfish.[188]

But the questions of morality aside, Greene's espionage and political novels were undoubtedly enhanced by his knowledge of the genre, by his experiences in wartime intelligence, and, perhaps most sharply, by his closeness to one of the most significant real-life spy dramas of the century — the unmasking of Kim Philby as a double agent. Greene had worked for Philby in the British Secret Intelligence Service during the latter stages of World War II and wrote the controversial, exculpatory foreword to Philby's memoir, *My Silent War* (1968), written from exile in Moscow. The Philby case, it seems, provided a touchstone for the kinds of issues that drew Greene toward the espionage genre: private loyalties in conflict with public duties, and belief and betrayal set amid a corrupting political world. In retrospect, one gets the feeling at times that Greene was specially created for espionage scenarios, those in which no one can trust anyone else. Moreover, whereas most enlightened people at the time were disgusted by the record of the Soviet Union, Greene appears to go out of his way to justify it. A close friend, the novelist Evelyn Waugh, thought this was just part of a vast master plan and noted that, "I think he [Greene] is a secret agent on our side and all his buttering up of the Russians is cover."[189]

While doubts as to Greene's political affiliations remain, it is certain that he was one of the more productive and knowledgeable writers of espionage fiction and made an essential contribution to the genre's postwar renaissance. But, for all his achievements, it was not Greene who set the postwar spy novel on a new course of popularity and established its dominant tones. This work instead was accomplished by a succession of writers, principally Ian Fleming, Len Deighton, and John Le Carré; the geopolitical circumstance of the Cold War; and, in particular, the various permutations drawn from post-Nazi Germany and the presumed menace of a potential Fourth Reich. These interrelated

188 Greene 1971.
189 Atkins 1984, 191-192.

themes creatively plumbed the depths of espionage in unique ways and directed the genre to become more of an instrument of political and social commentary.

Chapter 5. Post-World War II — Reality, Conspiracy, and Plot Development

> "The dream of the Lebensborn," said the American reverentially. "The breeding farms — estates actually, if I'm not to be mistaken, where the finest SS officers were bred to strong Teutonic women."
>
> "Eichmann had studies done. It was determined that the northern Germanic female had not only the finest bone structure in Europe and extraordinary strength, but a marked subservience to the male," interrupted the general.
>
> "The true superior race," concluded Lassiter admiringly. "Would that the dream had come true."
>
> "In a large measure it has," said Von Schnabe quietly.
>
> — Robert Ludlum, *The Apocalypse Watch*, 1995

By the end of World War II, espionage fiction had emerged as a distinct yet still evolving genre as a new generation of writers expanded the parameters defined by Maugham, Greene and Amber, and stewarded the genre in new directions. Character, place, incident, and plot still drove the genre, but the advent of the Cold War — and its attendant real world tensions, suspicions and intrigues — required a distinctive adjustment in both tone and complexity so as to maintain the requisite sense of reality. And while the stories retained their customary depictions of heroes and villains estranged by ideological and geopolitical factors, there emerged a growing sense — both feeding and feeding off of conspiracy theories — that the intelligence agencies of even one's own country were not to be trusted. Scholars examined "spy fiction" against the baseline of "spy reality," and in Germany and elsewhere in Europe there developed a substantial body of writing that drew upon the fiction of espionage to analyze and understand societal fears. This "social legitimization" by academia served a dual purpose: not only did it increase the popular acceptance of the genre, but it also compelled the serious spy novelist to take considerable efforts to ensure the accuracy of a story's political, technological, and psychological detail.[190]

Still, while the engagement with reality remained central to the evolution of espionage fiction, a certain Cold War specter began to course the genre in two, seemingly divergent, conspiracy theory themes. The first was directed to Hitler and post-World War II Nazi scenarios, while the second pondered the Soviet KGB and its husbandry of East Germany's Ministry for State Security — the Stasi.

The Conspiratorial View of History ~

In general, wars start when one nation moves into the territory of another; depressions occur when markets take unexpected downturns; inflations occur when prices are driven up by shortages; and revolutions start when the people, usually spontaneously, rise up to overthrow the existing governments. These are the traditional explanations of historical events. But this explanation of history leaves questions in the minds of some observers. What happens when events seemingly happen by accident? When there do not seem to be any apparent causes? Is it possible that government leaders and others planned these events and then orchestrated them to their desired conclusions? Is it possible that even the great catastrophes of history were part of this plan?[191]

There is an explanation of historical events that answers these last two questions in the affirmative. It is called the *conspiratorial view of history* and in it is the beginning of contemporary genre fiction. Franklin D. Roosevelt, who certainly saw many monumental events occur during his consecutive presidential administrations, has been quoted as saying: "In politics, nothing happens by accident. If it happens, you can

190 Winks 1998, xiii.
191 Epperson 1985, 6.

bet it was planned that way."[192] More succinctly, political events occur by design for reasons that are not generally made known to the people.

For the spy novelist the potential is obvious. If harmful events are indeed planned, it follows that the people who were about to suffer through the scheduled event would act to prevent the event from occurring if they knew about it in advance. These same people expect government to protect them from harmful events. If an event still occurs after the government officials had been expected to prevent it, the government officials have failed in their assigned duties. In this case, there are only two explanations as to why they failed: one, the event so overwhelmed them that it could not have been prevented; or, two, the event occurred because certain officials wanted it to occur.[193]

As a practical matter, it is all but impossible for the casual observer to believe that incredible events — such as a world war — could not have been prevented, as humane people of conscience do not allow such harmful events to occur. Taken a step further, if a planned and unwanted event is allowed to happen, those who planned the event would have to have acted in secret so as to prevent discovery of their plans by those who might be adversely affected. It is this same sphere of secrecy that becomes the medium for conspiracy theory, particularly as applied to contemporary genre fiction. The first task of a conspiracy, then, becomes that of convincing the people the conspiracy itself does not exist. This makes the task of uncovering the machinations of the conspiracy all the more difficult and sets the stage for the second major requirement of genre fiction: the introduction of a protagonist who will generally expose the conspiracy and resolve the issue at hand.[194]

In the spy novel, as in real life, there are generally three ways of exposing a conspiracy. One is for any of the participants in the conspiracy to break with it and to expose his or her involvement. This takes an extremely courageous individual and, while it may occur in fiction, its occurrence in real life is somewhat rarer. The second means of exposure involves individuals who have unknowingly participated in the con-

---

192 Roosevelt 2001.
193 Epperson 1985, 7.
194 Ibid.

spiratorial planning of an event but who did not realize it until later. These individuals, also a very small real world number, will expose the inner workings of the conspiracy at great peril to themselves. The final method of exposing a conspiracy is for a single investigator, or a small group of investigators, to uncover conspiratorial designs in the events of the past or seemingly unrelated events of the present, or, perhaps, a combination of both. This is the approach favored by most genre authors.[195]

As foundation, it is generally the perception of espionage novelists that a particular conspiracy could *conceivably* exist and, if so, that it is relatively large, deeply entrenched and therefore extremely powerful. Too, it is evil, working to achieve absolute and brutal rule over, for example, the free world, by using wars, depressions, inflations and revolutions to further its aims. And the conspiracy must normally have grand designs: to destroy all religion, all existing governments, and all traditional human institutions, and to build some enigmatic *new world order* upon the wreckage they have created. Finally, and most importantly, the conspiracy will be ruthless and will do everything it can to deny the charges of both those who seek to expose it and those who claim to have been a part of it. So, what, precisely, is conspiracy history? It is certainly not fact; but neither is it fiction. Perhaps the most functional definition would be to consider it the embodiment of fiction rooted in fact.[196]

In his 1966 book, *Tragedy and Hope*, Carroll Quigley proposed that small groups of individuals covertly influencing larger activities may well be extant:

> There does exist, and has existed for a generation, an international Anglophile network which operates, to some extent, in the way the radical right believes the Communists act. In fact, this network, which we may identify as the Round Table Groups, has no aversion to cooperating with the Communists, or any group, and frequently does so. I know of the operations of this network because I have studied it for twenty years and was permitted for two years, in the early 1960s, to examine its papers and secret records. I have no aversion to it or most of its aims, and have, for much of my life, been close to it and many of its instruments. I have objected, both in the past and recently, to a few of its poli-

---

195 Ibid., 8.
196 Ibid.

cies...but in general my chief difference of opinion is that it wishes to remain unknown, and I believe its role in history is significant enough to be known.[197]

That Quigley would think to make such a statement prompted no small measure of discomfort throughout the academic and international political communities. He was a respected scholar with impeccable academic credentials — he was educated at Harvard and Princeton and taught at the School of Foreign Service, Harvard, Yale, the Brookings Institute and the Foreign Service Institute of the US State Department — and he was the author of *The Evolution of Civilizations* (1961), a high respected and critically acclaimed book in which he sought to define the developmental pattern of civilizations.

But with *Tragedy and Hope* he claimed that an organization, variously titled the "Rhodes-Milner Group," the "Round Table," and just the "Milner Group," had virtual control over British foreign policy for much of the first half of this century when Britain was one of the world's leading powers.[198] The inner core of this group, the Round Table, was a secret society founded by the influential British colonial statesman Cecil Rhodes. Using Rhodes' money, this group set up the Round Table groups in the then British Dominions; in the Council on Foreign Relations in the US; in the network of Royal Institutes of International Affairs; and in the various Institutes of Pacific Relations. It also controlled *The Times* and the *Observer*, All Souls College at Oxford, the Rhodes Scholarship program and, according to Quigley, it alone was answerable for the destruction of the League of Nations, the British appeasement policies of the 1930s, and the conversion of the British Empire into a Commonwealth.[199]

These "gracious and cultivated men of somewhat limited social experience," as Quigley describes them, "constantly thought in terms of Anglo-American solidarity, of political partition and federation...and were convinced that they could gracefully civilise the Boers of South Africa, the Irish, the Arabs and the Hindus...and were largely respon-

---

197 Quigley 1966, 61.
198 In brief, Quigley believed that Western civilization had recycled itself three times based on feudalism, merchant capitalism, and industrial capitalism, respectively. Each expansion phase had kindled a conflict phase without, however, leading to a universal empire incorporating all or most of the civilization.
199 Ramsay 2000.

sible for the partition of Ireland, Palestine and India, and for the federations of South Africa, Central Africa and the West Indies."[200] Further to the point Quigley posited the existence of a far reaching financial and political conspiracy orchestrated by some of the most influential family names in British imperialist history: Rhodes, Rothschild, Milner, Smuts, Amery and Astor, among others, adding that these individuals desired "nothing less than to create a world system of financial control in private hands able to dominate the political system of each country and the economy of the world as a whole. The system [is] controlled in a feudal fashion by the central banks of the world acting in concert, by secret agreements arrived at in private meetings and conferences."[201]

In the end, despite his credentials, the book being published by a major firm, and its unusual page length and scope, *Tragedy and Hope* attracted only two insignificant, dismissive reviews from Quigley's peers, who noted that the 1300 pages carried no documentation or source references of any kind. The results, for Quigley, were disappointing. The American academic world berated the book and, having had no reviews, the book didn't sell, prompting Macmillan Publishers to destroy the plates from which the first edition had been printed. When the American writer Robert Eringer interviewed Quigley just before Quigley's death, Quigley warned him that writing about him and his book could get Eringer into trouble.[202] Notwithstanding, the one group of people who did take Quigley to heart were the conspiracy theorists of the radical right in America, for whom *Tragedy and Hope* became a kind of bible. Here was the proof, they believed, the academically respectable proof of the great conspiracy for which they had been searching. And, be it fact or fiction, *Tragedy and Hope* is great fodder for "fiction," if not academia.

Conspiracy theory has a long history in the Western world and has animated political culture from the early Republican period to the present, at times powerfully swaying popular opinion, and its influence grow. Since 1950s, an extraordinary number of writers have used expressions of paranoia and conspiracy theory to represent the insidious

---

200 Quigley 1966, 954.
201 Ibid., 324.
202 Ramsay 2000.

influence of postwar technologies, social organizations, and communication systems on human beings. Even non-espionage writers such as William S. Burroughs and Margaret Atwood, Thomas Pynchon and Joan Didion, and Kathy Acker and Don DeLillo have depicted individuals nervous about the ways large organizations might be somehow controlling their lives, influencing their actions, or even constructing their desires. Too, these same concerns are reflected in postwar films, television shows, and other media, which routinely posit conspiracies of astonishing size, depth, and complexity. The result? Sociological studies have shown that many people now simply assume that such plots are not only possible but are operative and determining forces in their own lives.[203]

"Someone once said that beneath or behind all political and cultural warfare lies a struggle between secret societies," states Ishmael Reed in *Mumbo Jumbo* (1973), where, as Brian McHale suggests, "he tries to convince us that beneath or behind all Western history lies the struggle between the Atonist Order and the agents of the Osirian-Dionysian mysteries." The latest manifestation of this particular conspiracy being the centuries-long struggle is the attempt by the white elite of the Wallflower Order to suppress jazz dancing in the 1920s. According to Reed, the Great Depression was nothing less that a conspiracy to keep Americans from being able to afford radios, thus restricting their access to subversive Black music, while the Second World War was an "extravaganza" staged by the Wallflower Order, an ancient conspiracy that controls most centers of power.[204]

History as paranoiac conspiracy theory is what Reed seemingly offers in *Mumbo Jumbo*, and it is a vision of history that he shares with many other postmodernist revisionist historical novelists including Thomas Pynchon, who, in his late-modernist text *V* (1963), makes his characters suspect that the perpetual crises of the twentieth century might be the fruit of some vast conspiracy operating in the "dark areas" of history. While in *The Crying of Lot* (1966) Pynchon confronts the protagonist with the possibility that America might be the battlefield for "a struggle between secret societies," it is in *Gravity's Rainbow* (1973)

---

203 Melley 2000, vii.
204 McHale 1996, 91.

that Pynchon achieves his most refined vision of secret history, un-covering layer upon layer of conspiracy behind the official historical facts of the Second World War. Is the war a plot by powerful men and the great international corporations and cartels? By the technologies themselves? By inscrutable and sinister forces from other places? The facts, as reinterpreted by Pynchon, might sustain one or more of these theories, but no final conclusion is possible; we are left with a kind of free-floating paranoia that remains subject to the powerful, sinister, and secret forces.[205]

Epperson suggests that the ultimate "motive" of conspiracy is "power," and that there are some who desire power more than even material goods, although the two frequently go together.[206] But why would successful individuals, particularly those of wealth and power, elect to join a conspiracy?[207] The answer, according to conspiracy theo-rists, is actually quite the reverse of the question: Those involved with conspiracy became illustrious primarily because they were part of the conspiracy.[208]

Taken a bit further, this seems to mover closer to exemplifying Lord Acton's oft quoted: "Power tends to corrupt and absolute power cor-rupts absolutely. Great men are almost always bad men, even when they exercise influence and not authority: still more when you super-add the tendency or the certainty of corruption by authority. There is no worse heresy than that the office sanctifies the holder of it."[209] And some of those who seek power will indeed be corrupted by it, and will indeed be willing to intentionally cause depressions, revolutions, and wars to further their desire for more power. When viewed from this perspective, the corrupting nature of power's pursuit explains why the moral mind of an individual who neither desires power over others, nor even understands the desire for such power, cannot fathom why pow-

---

205 Ibid.
206 Ralph Epperson has been researching the conspiratorial view of history for some 30 years. He has written or produced two books on the subject, *The Unseen Hand* and *The New World Order*.
207 Epperson 1985, 9.
208 Ibid., 10.
209 Himmelfarb 1952, 161.

er-seekers would want to create human misery through these same de-pressions, revolutions, and wars.[210]

So, it appears, the principal motive of conspiracy has been reason-ably defined: it is power. And perhaps at no time in recent history has this realization of power — along with its attendant ruthlessness — emerged more absolute than during the eras of Nazi Germany and the Soviet occupation of Eastern Europe during the Cold War, both of which have provided dramatic backdrop to the evolution of the spy novel.

THE NAZI FACTOR -

With few exceptions, the employment of Nazis in contemporary genre fiction is a seamless application that combines the flexibility of conspiracy theory with the interpretation of selected historical events. The circumstance of World War II in Europe and its historical hand-maidens: the Holocaust, the Nuremberg War Crimes Trials and the Cold War, have provided us — in the Western sense — with a pro-found sense of authenticity that is further enhanced by gruesome visual images and repugnant documentary evidence. Yet the history is real, and, being real, it has served as the catalyst that inspired any number of changes to the European political fabric following World War II.

Upon the cessation of hostilities in Europe, official policies, the media and the public quickly achieved consensus as to the malevo-lence of Nazism. Still, there remains the lingering issue of fugitive war criminals and the whispered conversations relating events — real and imagined — of post-World War II Western spy agencies, particularly the American CIA, having cooperated with former Nazis. Is this true? Undoubtedly, yes, but it remains unclear to what extent. The actual operational particulars mostly remain classified under the provisions of Great Britain's *Official Secrets Act* and are specifically exempted from re-lease under the American *Freedom of Information Act*. Add to these the se-crecy and paranoia of the Cold War and suspicions of some new world order clandestinely planning this or that havoc against society — be their designs international or directed to a single mission activity —

---

210 Epperson 1985, 10.

and one is very near the juncture of what had been defined to be "cultural paranoia."[211] And it is this very paranoia that may be selectively exploited by the contemporary spy novelist.

History is a construct, like theater: a human creation that intensifies (but thereby inevitably falsifies) experience.[212] For the espionage novelist this concept appears particularly valid for, in the vast majority of cases, the fundamental premises of the espionage story — again, character, place, incident and plot — are derived from historical perception rather than from the unbiased analysis of public facts, therein permitting no small measure of creative interpretation and selective extrapolation. In concert with this perception is the vague awareness that some measure of Nazi threat remains and will once again manifest itself in the guise of a sinister cabal rising from some political nether region and eventually holding sway over legitimate authority. To spy novelists — particularly those employing Nazis as villains — this provides an extremely fertile domain, for there exists a large body of work upon which to base one's story: again, the conspiratorial view of history.

The Nazi regime defines the essence of conspiratorial history: covert alliances, layers of secrecy, and the lines of reality mired in political intrigue, disinformation and selected interpretations of historical events. A case in point is the relationship between Nazi Germany, the Western banking community, and the chemical cartel called I.G. Farben.[213] Without I.G. Farben's immense petrochemical production facilities, its far reaching research, varied technical experience and overall concentration of economic power, Germany would not have been in a position to start its aggressive war in September 1939.[214]

I.G. Farben enjoyed substantial financial strength due to the enormous economic power of its principal underwriters: America's Wall Street banks. For, without the capital supplied by Wall Street, there would have been no I.G. Farben in the first place, and almost certainly no Adolf Hitler and World War II.[215] I.G. Farben had its beginning in

---

211 Hofstadter 1998, 221.

212 Janick 1995, 160.

213 This is an abbreviation of the complete corporate name: *Interssen Gemeinschaft Farben.*

214 Borkin 1978, 1

215 Sutton 1979, 33.

1924, when American banker Charles Dawes arranged a series of foreign loans totaling $800 million to consolidate various large chemical
and steel corporations into cartels, one of which was I.G. Farben. As
orchestrated by Dawes, three Wall Street banking houses — Dillon,
Read & Co.; Harris, Forbes & Co.; and National City — handled three-
quarters of the loans used to create the cartels.[216] American support for
Farben continued as Henry Ford, among others, merged his German
assets with those of Farben in 1928.

The prominence of I.G. Farben in the plans of the German Nazi
Party should not be underestimated. A Farben-dominated company
produced the chemical *Zyklon B*, the lethal gas utilized by Hitler's ex-
terminators at Auschwitz, Buchenwald and a number of other concentration camps.[217] While, from a humanitarian aspect, the application
of *Zyklon B* is indeed significant, in the broader operational sense the
real importance of Farben to Hitler's war efforts came in the utilization
of the process known as hydrogenation — the production of gasoline
from coal.[218]

Germany had no native gasoline production capabilities and this
was one of the principal reasons it lost World War I. But Germany did
possess large quantities of coal. Further, it was a German scientist who
first discovered the process of converting coal into gasoline in 1909, but
the technology was not completely developed during World War I. In
August 1927, Standard Oil agreed to embark on a cooperative program
of research and development of the hydrogenation process to refine the
oil necessary for Germany to prepare for World War II.[219] The cooperative agreement bore fruit and in 1929 the two companies signed a cartel
agreement containing two key objectives:

    1. To grant Standard Oil one-half of all rights to the hydrogenation
       process in all countries of the world except Germany; and

---

216 Quigley terms the Dawes Plan, "largely a J.P. Morgan production" (Quigley 1966,
308).

217 I. G. Farben, being a chemical company even before it was merged with other
chemical companies to form the cartel, had considerable expertise in this area,
as it was also the producer of the chlorine gas deployed by the Axis powers during World War I.

218 The various international financial relationships that existed between the
Rothschild and Morgan banking houses are discussed in Stanley Jackson's
book, *J.P. Morgan*, New York: Stein and Day, 1983.

219 Epperson 1985, 267.

2. To prohibit competition with each other in the fields of chemistry and petroleum products. In the future, if Standard Oil wished to enter the broad field of industrial chemicals or drugs, it would do so only as a partner of I.G. Farben. I.G. Farben, in turn, agreed never to enter the field of petroleum except as a joint venture with Standard Oil.[220]

The cartel agreement was critical to the German war effort because, by the end of the World War II, Germany was producing about seventy-five percent of its fuel synthetically. But even more significant was the fact that these plants were not the subject of Allied bombing raids and, by the war's end, twenty-five to thirty of its refineries were still operating with only approximately fifteen percent damage. Why were the German refineries not targeted for bombing? According to conspiracy historians, America was protecting its investment. And although there appears to be little, if any, documentary proof that the United States was deliberately avoiding German petrochemical facilities for financial reasons, the very possibility — again drawn from the subtle blending of fact and fiction — that it *could* have occurred provides the espionage novelist with numerous plausible plot scenarios.[221]

A second, particularly lucrative area for espionage novelists directs itself to actual Nazi intelligence activity during, and shortly after, World War II. To illustrate the considerable potential for fictional extrapolation, the case of Nazi general Reinhard Gehlen appears worthy of consideration, for the mystery surrounding Gehlen and his vast network of opportunistic spies made a huge impact on a half century of American espionage. It is also a representative of the moral compromises the United States made as the clear line between good and evil during World War II blurred into the much murkier, yet equally terrifying, Cold War.[222]

The Gehlen scenario is the *factual* account of the relationship between two World War II generals — one Russian, the other German — and serves as perhaps the best example of how actual historical events can appear more fictional than authentic, while simultaneously illus-

---

220 Griffin 1974, 254.

221 In 1979, Steve Shagan's industrial espionage novel *The Formula* concerned itself with the "Genesis" formula, the secret for synthetic fuel developed by the Germans in World War II. The big oil companies want the formula suppressed because it would allow cheap gasoline to be made from widely available coal.

222 Fritz 2001.

trating the fine line that can exist between fiction and non-fiction.[223] The Russian general is Andrei Vlasov, an Army officer secretly working with an extensive anti-Bolshevist — and anti-Stalin — spy ring. Vlasov joined his forces with the advancing Germans during the invasion of the Ukraine, where Russian forces antagonistic to Stalin and anxious to overthrow the Bolsheviks had collected. Vlasov commanded the so-called Army of Liberation, a full division of troops fighting under the flag of Great White Russia and who supported the restoration of the Czar.[224]

The second general is Reinhard Gehlen, the director of Hitler's powerful anti-Soviet intelligence apparatus. Unbeknownst to Hitler, the practical basis of the great success of Gehlen's Soviet intelligence system was his personal relationship with Andrei Vlasov. Through Vlasov, Gehlen had access to the Russian anti-Bolshevist underground network that had long since penetrated, if not *de facto* controlled, key departments of the Soviet regime. At a moment in their invasion when the Nazis still thought themselves on the brink of victory over the Soviets, Gehlen proposed to Hitler that Vlasov be made the head of the forthcoming provisional government. Hitler declined, presumably from fear of Vlasov's power, but the relationship between Gehlen and Vlasov and their spy systems remained intact even after the defeat of the *Wehrmacht* in the Battle of Stalingrad in the winter of 1942-43.

By Christmas 1944, Gehlen had reached the belief Germany's cause was hopeless. Against the certainty of national defeat, he determined his only personal choice lay between surrender to the Russians or surrender to the Americans. Four months later, in April 1945, with the Russian army closing on Berlin, Gehlen gathered together with his top aides in a hotel room in Bad Elster, Saxony. There, they made the decision to align themselves with the Americans and developed their plan. They stripped their archives of the intelligence information that would be most useful to them in subsequent negotiations, burned tons of other documents, and then clandestinely stored their intelligence cache in

---

223 Gehlen was also one of the prime targets of a commission that President Bill Clinton appointed in 1999 to oversee the release of intelligence records under the *Nazi War Crimes Disclosure Act*.

224 Vlasov was captured by the Americans after the war. He was turned over to the Soviets for "trial" and perfunctorily executed.

the Bavarian Redoubt, overlooked by a chalet that Gehlen's foresight had long before provisioned. Safe with his forty top aides and his buried spy treasures, Gehlen settled down to await the Americans.

By May Day 1945, the Red Army was in Berlin and Hitler was thought to be dead. Three weeks later, columns of the American 101st Airborne Division moved up the valley below Gehlen's mountain fortress. Gehlen's aides descended from the upper slopes to present themselves for capture and arrange an appointment for the capture of their commander, the highest-ranking German officer and Hitler's only staff general yet to make his way to safety in American hands.[225]

Gehlen found himself treated like a visiting dignitary and some three months later arrived in Washington DC, in the uniform of a United States Army general, and flown there in the personal aircraft of General Walter Bedell Smith, Eisenhower's chief of staff. In a series of secret meetings with senior American intelligence luminaries — such as future CIA Director Allen Dulles and General William J. Donovan, Director of the Office of Strategic Services (OSS), the lineal predecessor of the CIA — Gehlen detailed his proposed "surrender conditions." It was to be a classic case of *quid pro quo*.[226]

Postwar Europe, Gehlen opined, was certain to become center stage for the next major international confrontation — that between the United States and the Soviet Union. Based upon his experience, the Soviets, he confided, were well-prepared for this new showdown from an intelligence standpoint. The Americans were not. The Russians possessed an expert spy network in Western Europe and America, but the Americans did not have a spy network of any kind or quality in Central Europe and Russia. Did that not put the Americans at an important disadvantage in the forthcoming struggles? And where and how could the Americans procure the needed capability? Recruiting and training a corps of Russian and Central European intelligence

---

225 Oglesby 1976, 40.

226 Gehlen was of course not the only high-ranking Nazi offering the United States "deals" at the end of the war. In April 1944, for example, agents of Heinrich Himmler — the director of the SS and a close Hitler confidant — were floating "separate peace" balloons all over Europe. In one offer, Himmler would turn over to the United States the German treasury of intelligence data on Japan if the United States would stall the war in France and enable the Nazis to put more into their struggle with Russia.

agents and building a network of reliable sources and experts from the ground up would take years, possibly even generations. The Americans agreed with Gehlen, to which Gehlen then presented the solution. His own intelligence apparatus was still intact within the collapsing Nazi government, and remained capable of delivering large masses of high-quality intelligence data on all aspects of Soviet life.

Gehlen's overture suggested the Americans simply acquire his organization and insert it into the void in their own intelligence system, as though it were one of the spoils of the war. Gehlen could plausibly guarantee his network's unmatched and unbending loyalty to the cause of anti-Bolshevism, and the intelligence cache he had buried in the Bavarian Redoubt would not only provide immediate information but would also present a foretaste of secret knowledge to come. To acquire the material, the Americans had to meet Gehlen's four conditions:

1. Gehlen was to have complete autonomy within his organization and total control over its activities. The Americans would tell him what they wanted and they would get it, satisfaction guaranteed, but they would know nothing of the process by which Gehlen acquired the information.

2. The Americans would agree to employ Gehlen's network only against the USSR and the East European satellites.

3. When a new German government was established, the Americans would constitutionally install the Gehlen organization as the new government's central intelligence agency and concurrently cancel all of outstanding Gehlen commitments to the United States. Gehlen, of course, would become director of the new agency.

4. The Americans would never require Gehlen to do anything he considered against German national interests. He even reserved the right to approve any American liaison officers assigned to him.

Eventually, the Americans agreed, creating a situation wherein, even as the United States was publicly proclaiming a policy of unconditional German surrender, Gehlen's extraordinary conditions quietly were being met as his organization was established at the very core and seat of the American system of foreign intelligence under the direct control of Allen Dulles' Secret Intelligence Branch of the OSS.

By the time of the 1948 evolution of the OSS into the CIA, Gehlen found himself enjoying a close personal relationship with Dulles as his organization, to all intents and purposes, became the CIA's department of Russian and East European affairs. But it was not to end there. After the formation of NATO, it became the official NATO intelligence organization and, soon thereafter, as per Gehlen's third condition, his organization was installed as the core, with himself as director, of the West German CIA, the *Bundesnachtendienst*.

While further examination of Gehlen's activities is not indicated, a consideration of the scenario through the eyes of a spy novelist raises numerous possibilities for this is truly the "stuff" of contemporary espionage fiction: One of Hitler's most senior generals — the exclusive purveyor of Nazi intelligence on Russia — is disguised as an American general and spirited to Washington DC in the personal aircraft of the supreme allied commander's chief of staff. With covert American support, he first becomes head of a division of the American OSS and CIA, then the principal intelligence official for NATO, and finally the head of the West German intelligence agency where, conceivably, he and his staff held more influence over Western postwar perceptions than even a German victory could have given them.[227] Yet this is precisely how it came to pass that a Czarist spy ring, inside a Nazi spy ring, took up inner seats in the American foreign intelligence apparatus at the precise moment that this same apparatus was beginning to come forward as a major player in the relentless intelligence pursuits of the Cold War.

When considering the various Nazi-related conspiracy scenarios available to the spy novelist, one can certainly not ignore the specter of Adolf Hitler who, perhaps above all others, patently exhibits the historical symmetry between power and conspiracy. His megalomania was legend, while at the same time he emerges in the guise of a conspiracy within a conspiracy with the lines of reality mired in layer after layer of occultism, international banking associations and political intrigues, a fluid state of historical affairs that, for the spy novelist in search of a story line, is remarkably lucrative.[228]

According to conspiracy historians, the inspiration of Nazism — and therefore World War II — began in 1919 when Hitler joined a se-

---

227 Gehlen's career and influence spanned the Cold War. While in retirement, he was brought to testify in the sensational 1974 West German spy scandal that brought down West German Chancellor Willy Brandt.

228 The Hitler conspiracy novels will be discussed in Chapter 7.

cret organization called the Thule Society, for in this group he found the distorted beliefs that were later to guide him in his control of the German government.[229] Formed in 1918, the Thule Society was originally founded by an enigmatic man named Rudolf Blauer, who held a Turkish passport and practiced *sufi* meditation. Blauer dabbled in astrology and was also an admirer of Guido von List and particularly of Jorg Lanz von Liebenfels, who, like von List, was pathologically anti-Semitic.[230] Blauer went by the name of Rudolf Freiherr von Seboottendorf and was very wealthy, although the origin of his fortune — or for that matter, why he chose to be known by another name — is unknown.

The emblem of the Thule Society depicted a German dagger over a reversed swastika of curved legs inscribed in a circle and, to its members, the sun played a key role as a sacred symbol of the Aryans, in contrast to the moon, which was revered by the Semitic peoples. Drawn from this, Hitler came to see the Jewish people, with their black hair and swarthy complexions, as the dark side of the human species, whilst the blond and blue-eyed Aryans constituted the light side of humanity. It would be a belief that would later play out with horrific consequences when Hitler undertook to extirpate from the material world what he believed to be "impure elements."[231]

---

229 The name "Thule" itself was taken from a legendary island in the far north, similar to Atlantis, purportedly the center of a lost, high-level civilization. But not all secrets of that civilization had been completely destroyed. Those that remained were being guarded by ancient, highly intelligent beings similar to the "Masters" of Theosophy or the White Brotherhood. The truly initiated could establish contact with these beings by means of mystical rituals and the "Masters" or "Ancients" allegedly would be able to endow the initiated with supernatural strength. With this guidance and, with the help of these energies, the goal of the initiated was to create a race of "Aryan stock" supermen who would exterminate all inferior races.

230 Guido von List was an Austrian mystic born in Vienna. He claimed to have visions in which he was initiated into the sacred traditions of ancient Teutonic clans. The visions allegedly revealed to him an ancient Nordic religion that worshiped the god Woten who acquired the secret of the runes. Jorg Lanz von Liebenfels was a defrocked monk who combined von List's teachings with his own interest in Eugenics and created a new doctrine that he termed "Theozoology." He claimed that the Atlantean's fourth root race [taken from Madame Blavatsky's seven root races] had, after thousands of years, allegedly interbred with beasts and were now separated into two races, one pure Aryan and one into a species of beasts. Due to this interbreeding, the Atlantean's [Aryan's] psychic power had reduced to nothing.

231 Angebert 1974, 4.

If anything, the Thule Society was *not* an organization for the "common man," as its membership included judges, police chiefs, attorneys, university professors, industrialists, physicians, scientists, as well as members of any number of influential aristocratic and bourgeois families. When the Nationalist Socialist German Workers Party (NSDAP) — the lineal predecessor to the Nazi Party — came into its own (c. 1920), its central committee and forty original members were all drawn from the Thule Society, which by that time had become the most powerful occult society in Germany.[232] In addition to Hitler, Thule Society members who would rise to prominence first in the NSDAP and later in the Nazi Party were Max Amann, director of the Nazi publishing house *Eher Verlag*; Hans Frank, Reich Minister and Governor-General of the occupied Polish Territories; Rudolf Hess, SS General and Deputy Fuhrer; Alfred Rosenberg, Reich Minister for the Occupied Eastern Territories; and Gottfried Feder, Hitler's economic advisor.

However — and again according to conspiracy theorists — it not just the fellowship of the Thule Society and its occultist-political intrigues that gave Hitler the support he needed to become the leader of the German government. There were additional, perhaps more personal sources of Hitler's mindset. And this, it seems, transitions Hitler from one conspiracy — that drawn from the Thule Society and the origins of Nazism — to the next conspiracy: the Rothschild connection.

In 1943 Walter Langer, a noted psychoanalyst, conducted a psychological analysis of Hitler entitled *The Mind of Adolf Hitler* which, to the astonishment of everyone who had access to the document, proposed that Hitler was himself one-quarter Jewish and the grandson of a Rothschild.[233] In the classified OSS report, Langer noted that there was a great deal of confusion in studying Hitler's family tree, much of it due to the fact that the name has been spelled in various ways: Hitler, Hidler, Hiedler, and Huettler. Langer concluded that it seemed reasonable to suppose, however, that it is fundamentally the same name spelled in

---

232 Ravenscroft 1973, 102.

233 Walter Langer conducted his psychological analysis of Adolf Hitler at the behest of the American Office of Strategic Services, c1943. Collaborating with Langer were Professor Henry A. Murr, Harvard Psychological Clinic; Dr. Ernst Kris, New School for Social Research; and Dr. Bertram D. Lawin, New York Psychoanalytic Institute.

various ways by different members of what was basically an illiterate peasant family. Adolf Hitler himself signed his name Hittler on his first Party membership blanks, and his sister usually spelled her name as Hiedler. Another element of confusion is introduced by the fact that Adolf's mother's mother was also named Hitler, which later became the family name of his father. Some of this confusion is dissipated, however, when it is realized that Adolf's parents had a common ancestor (father's grandfather and mother's great-grandfather), who came from the culturally backward Waldviertel district of Austria.

Adolf's father, Alois Hitler, was the illegitimate son of Maria Anna Schicklgruber. It was generally supposed that the father of Alois Hitler was a Johann Georg Hiedler, a miller's assistant. Alois, however, was not legitimized, and he bore his mother's name until he was forty years of age when he changed it to Hitler. Just why this was done is not clear, but it was generally said among the villagers that it was necessary in order to obtain a legacy. Where the legacy came from is unknown. One could suppose that Johann Georg Hiedler relented on his deathbed and left an inheritance to his illegitimate son together with his name. It seems strange, however, that he did not legitimize the son when he married Anna Schicklgruber thirty-five years earlier. Why the son chose to take the name Hitler instead of Hiedler, if this is the case, is also a mystery that has remained unsolved. Unfortunately, the date of the death of Hiedler has not been established and consequently no researcher has been able to relate these two events in time. Still, a peculiar series of events, prior to Adolf Hitler's birth, furnishes ample food for speculation.

There are some people who seriously doubt that Johann Georg Hiedler was the father of Alois. Langer observed that other researchers claimed that Chancellor Dollfuss of Austria had ordered the Austrian police to conduct a thorough investigation into the Hitler family. As a result of this investigation a secret document was prepared that proved that Maria Anna Schicklgruber was living in Vienna at the time she conceived. At that time she was employed as a servant in the home of Baron Rothschild where, presumably, she and the Baron had entertained some manner of illicit liaison. As soon as the Rothschild family discovered her pregnancy she was sent back to her home in Spital, where Alois was born. If it is true that one of the Rothschilds is the real father of Alois Hitler, it would make Adolf a quarter Jew. According to Langer's report, Adolf Hitler knew of the existence of the Austrian document and the incriminating evidence it contained. In order to obtain it he precipitated events in Austria and initiated the assassination of Dollfuss. But Hitler failed to obtain the document at that time since Dollfuss had secreted it and had told Kurt von Schuschnigg, the Austrian Minister of Justice, of its whereabouts so that in the event of his death the independence of Austria would remain assured.[234] Those who lend credulity to this story point out several factors that seem to favor its plausibility:

1. That it is unlikely that the miller's assistant in a small village in this district would have very much to leave in the form of a legacy.
2. That it is strange that Johann Hiedler should not claim the boy until thirty-five years after he had married the mother, and after the mother had died.
3. That if the legacy were left by Hiedler on the condition that Alois take his name, it would not have been possible for him to change it to Hitler.
4. That the intelligence and behavior of Alois, as well as that of his two sons, is completely out of keeping with that usually found in Austrian peasant families. They point out that their ambitiousness and extraordinary political intuition are much more in harmony with the Rothschild tradition.
5. That Alois Schicklgruber left his home village at an early age to seek his fortune in Vienna, where his mother had worked.
6. That it would be peculiar for Alois Hitler, while working as a customs official in Braunau, to choose a Jew named Print, of Vienna, to act as Adolf's godfather unless he felt some kinship with the Jews himself.

Several stories of this general character are in circulation and while it is certainly a very intriguing hypothesis — and much of Adolf's later behavior could be explained in rather easy terms on this basis — it remains largely unproven. In any event, Maria Anna Schicklgruber died when Alois was five years of age. When he was thirteen Alois left the

---

234 Dollfuss was assassinated during the unsuccessful Nazi Putsch of July 25, 1934. This was Hitler's attempt to seize top Austrian government officials and force the appointment of a Nazi-dominated government.

Waldviertel and went to Vienna, where he learned to be a cobbler. The next twenty-three years of his life are largely unaccounted for, although it seems probable that during this time he joined the army and had perhaps been advanced to the rank of noncommissioned officer. His service in the army may have helped him to enter the civil service as customs official later on.[235]

It is, at least theoretically, possible that Hitler discovered his Jewish background and his relation to the Rothschilds and, aware of their enormous power to make or break European governments, reestablished contact with the family. This would explain, albeit partially, the enormous support he received from the international banking fraternity, closely entwined with the Rothschild family, as he rose to power. One thing, however, is certain — Hitler instigated World War II by moving first into Austria. Why Austria? Two reasons, according to conspiracy theory, have been put forward: first, he sought to silence Chancellor Dollfuss who, from the Austrian police, knew that Hitler was a descendant of the Rothschilds; and second, Hitler wished to remove all traces of his ancestry from the Austrian records.[236] However, as pointed out in the postscript in Langer's book, the point of overriding psychological and historical importance is not whether it is true that Hitler had a Jewish grandfather but whether he believed that it might be true. If he did so believe, then this fact alone doubtless shaped both his personality and his public policy.[237]

The final and perhaps most controversial conspiracy surrounding Adolf Hitler is, of course, the mystery surrounding his demise for, even in death, the Fuhrer remained controversial and mysterious. After the war, the parents of SS General Otto Fegelein, for instance, assured an American counterintelligence agent that a courier had brought a message from their son that he and Hitler were safe and well in Argentina. Stalin also professed doubt. He told Harry Hopkins, a Franklin Roosevelt confidant, that Hitler's end struck him as dubious. Hitler had surely escaped and was in hiding with Bormann. This version became Soviet history until 1968 when a Soviet journalist, Lev Bezymen-

235 Langer 1972, 111-113.
236 Epperson 1985, 266.
237 Ibid., 234.

ski, published a book revealing that the Russians had found the bodies of Adolf Hitler and his mistress Eva Braun outside the bunker on May 4, 1945.

As evidence, Bezymenski included an autopsy report of the Forensic Medical Commission of the Red Army, which stated that splinters of a poison ampoule had been found in the Fuhrer's mouth and there was no bullet hole in the skull. In other words, the Soviets implied that Hitler had taken a cowardly route to death. Moreover, added the report, he had but one testicle — a conclusion made much of by some psycho-historians despite reports from three doctors who had examined Hitler indicating his genitalia were normal. The long-delayed Soviet revelation was received with some suspicion. Although the detailed report was authenticated by five pathologists and experts in forensic medicine, it was supported only by photographic evidence of Hitler's corpse. The remains themselves, Bezymenski admitted, had been completely burned and their ashes strewn to the wind.

Skeptics wondered why Stalin had spread the story in 1945 that Hitler had escaped when he knew the body had been found. They were not at all convinced by Bezymenski's explanation that, first of all, it had been resolved not to publish the results of the forensic medical report but to hold it in reserve in case someone might try to slip into the role of the Fuhrer, presumably saved by some sort of miracle. And, secondly, that it had been further resolved to continue the investigations in order to exclude any possibility of error or deliberate deception. Of course neither reason accounts for the wait of twenty-three years, nor was any explanation given for the destruction of the remains.

Pictures of the Hitler's corpse's *dentures* had been kept on file and in 1972 Dr. Reidar Soggnaes, a dental forensic expert from the University of California at Los Angeles, discovered that these teeth exactly matched those in the X-ray head plates of Hitler taken in 1943. This hard evidence, Dr. Soggnaes told the 6th International Meeting of Forensic Sciences at Edinburgh, proved beyond doubt that Hitler was dead and that the Soviets had autopsied the right body. But they were dentures, the conspiracy theorists countered. Could not they be duplicated? And where was the proof that Hitler had not shot himself? The skull proving that there was no bullet hole had been conveniently destroyed. Moreover, none of the eyewitnesses in the bunker had noticed the telltale discolorations of cyanide on Hitler's lips; and only one empty poison capsule had been found, that having been presumably used by Hitler's consort Eva Braun.[238]

Ultimately, the forensic evidence raised more questions than they answered: a fact immediately seized upon by the conspiracy theorists who responded with any number of their own interpretations and "statements of fact." For example:

1. That in 1974 on a Canadian Broadcasting Corporation program called *As It Happens*, Dr. Soggnaes himself said that Hitler had ordered a special plane to leave from Berlin with all medical and dental records, especially X-rays, of all top Nazis, for an unknown destination. He said that the dental records used to identify Hitler's body were drawn from memory by a dental assistant, who disappeared and was never found.

2. That an editorial in *Zig Zag* (Santiago, Chile, 1948), stated that on April 30th, 1945, Flight Captain Peter Baumgart took Adolf Hitler, his wife Eva Braun, as well as a few loyal friends by plane from Tempelhof Airport to Tondern in Denmark (still German controlled). From Tondern, they took another plane to Kristiansund in Norway (also German controlled). From there they joined a submarine convoy sailing for South America.

3. That the Jewish writer Michael Bar-Zohar in *The Avengers* wrote that in 1943 Nazi Admiral Karl Doenitz had declared: "The German U-boat fleet is proud to have made an earthly paradise, an impregnable fortress for the Fuhrer, somewhere in the world." He did not say in what part of the world it existed, but fairly obviously it was in South America.

4. That a German writer named Mattern said that Admiral Doenitz told a graduating class of naval cadets in Kiel in 1944: "The German Navy has still a great role to play in the future. The German Navy knows all the hiding places for the Navy to take the Fuhrer to, should the need arise. There he can prepare his last measures in complete quiet."[239]

While the Hitler themes are perhaps the most ambitious in their scope, when considered in concert with the innumerable other World War II Nazi conspiracy scenarios such as the Gehlen and I. G. Far-

---

238 Toland 1976, 1007-1008.

239 While there have been are numerous "Hitler Living in South America" scenarios proposed in books and articles, the four cited here are drawn from the conspiracy website http://www.think-aboutit.com/Omega/files/ that, in addition to a *Hitler Alive!* chapter, also offers chapters on other popular Nazi conspiracy themes such as Rudolf Hess and Secret German Space Base, Nazi Bases in Antarctica and German Flying Discs.

ben affairs, it is clear to see that the Nazi era offers what can only be described as a body of historically plausible — or at least remotely conceivable — scenarios that, if suitably sketched against the historical record, are readily available for exploitation by contemporary spy novelists.

THE STASI FACTOR ·

Founded in geopolitical reality, the specter of East Germany emerges as one of the major themes in the evolution of post-World War II espionage fiction, particularly as seen in the works of Deighton and Le Carré. Immediately after World War II, there was a marked perception that Soviet truculence posed a threat to the postwar recovery of Western Europe. However, due in large part to American economic assistance through the Marshall Plan, Western Europe avoided the economic chaos that the Communists could have exploited through subversion and revolution. But full economic recovery in these nations remained hampered by fears that Soviet Russia, whose armed strength had increased rather than decreased after the war, would take by invasion what Communist agents were unable to subvert from within. Although the United States, at that time, still possessed a nuclear monopoly, Western Europeans feared that a Soviet overland attack could overrun Western Europe in less than a week. They recognized their own collective military impotence and doubted that America would react in time to prevent a *fait accompli*.[240]

In 1948, the communists took power in Czechoslovakia and made alarming gains in the polls in Italy and France.[241] To deal with similar issues, in April 1949 a treaty was signed to establish a North Atlantic Treaty Organization (NATO). The signatories agreed to settle disputes by peaceful means and to develop their individual and collective capacity to resist armed attack, to regard an attack on one as an attack on all, and to take necessary action to repel the attack. While these fears of war swirled across the world stage, East and West intelligence agencies struggled in a fog of experimentation and frustration, seeking on the one hand to infiltrate the ranks of their opposite numbers and on

240 Dupuy 1986, 1257.
241 Boyle 1979, 247.

the other hand to keep their opposite numbers from infiltrating their own ranks.

The Soviet Union was caught off guard by Western Europe's prompt acceptance of the Marshall Plan — as well as the NATO agreement — and began to redouble its efforts to regain the upper hand. A permanently weakened Germany could still become a Kremlin pawn and a Germany gradually unified from within by Soviet manipulation became Stalin's prime objective in the West towards the end of 1947. For propaganda purposes, an Eastern counterpart to the Marshall Plan was launched for the benefit of the Soviet satellites. A second aim was to cut off the trickle of trade that had started to flow between the two halves of divided Europe.

Allied control of Berlin and of Germany as a whole had been hampered since the Potsdam agreement and by the Soviet policy of treating their zone and city sector as if these were exclusively Russian territory. The result was that the political, military and intelligence strategies of all nations were decisively influenced by the confrontation between the United States and the Soviet Union. The two superpowers towered over the other nations of the world, and the most important strategic fact of life for each was the existence and power of the other. The friction and discord which resulted from this confrontation came to be termed the "Cold War" and although, after some time, the grimness of the political situation was somewhat ameliorated by American and Soviet efforts to achieve a form of peaceful coexistence — which both sides preferred to call *détente* — the confrontation was still the major factor of world affairs, and relations were frequently chilly, particularly in post-World War II Germany, and even more particularly in Berlin where, in a geographic sense, the two opposing philosophies of East and West actually abutted one another.

To protect its interests in Eastern Germany, the Soviet KGB promoted the establishment of East Germany's Ministry for State Security: the secret police apparatus known as the Stasi. As a direct beneficiary of Soviet tutelage and support — as well as serving as a *de facto* arm of the KGB — the Stasi soon emerged as one of the most comprehensive internal security operations of the Cold War. The Stasi closely monitored the movements of the entire population, compiling information on those whose thoughts, speech or actions were in any way out of step with Communist Party dictates.

The Stasi kept close tabs on all potential subversives, to the point of even collecting scent samples from people by wiping bits of cloth on objects they had touched. These samples were stored in airtight glass containers and special dogs were trained to track down the person's scent. The agency was authorized to conduct secret smear campaigns against anyone it judged to be a threat. This might include sending anonymous letters and making anonymous phone calls to blackmail the targeted person, and torture was an accepted tool of information acquisition. Elsewhere, in addition to its programs for internal repression, the Stasi actively engaged in international espionage, terrorism and terrorist training, involvement in narcotics and art theft, and special operations in Latin America. [242]

For the spy novelist, the seductiveness of East-West intelligence operations in Cold War Germany, coupled with the Stasi-KGB connection as well as the various intrigues surrounding the Berlin Wall and its distinctive imprint on the times, offered a promising venue. The fleeting sense of optimism spawned by victory in World War II had — particularly as related to intelligence activities — given way to the disillusionment and distrust of the Cold War and the deep fears generated by nuclear proliferation.

In order to more accurately reflect the cynicism and suspicion of the era, the genre once again evolved, in general becoming increasingly introspective and delving even deeper into the human element as a more sophisticated authenticity began to cloak plot and character development. As this trend took hold, it was often genuinely difficult to know who was an enemy and who was not and, in some cases, once the enemy had been established there was a powerful tendency to admire and respect and, finally, even to love him. People who are paid to hate

---

242 The Stasi built an astonishingly widespread network of informants and researchers estimate that out of a population of 16 million, 400,000 people actively cooperated with the Stasi. The Stasi kept files on up to 6 million East German citizens — one-third of the entire population — and operated with broad power and remarkable attention to detail. All phone calls from the West were monitored, as was all mail. Similar surveillance was routine domestically. Every factory, social club, and youth association was infiltrated and many East Germans were persuaded or blackmailed into informing on their own families.

and kill others, that is to say professionals, have a way of getting on the best of terms with those they are supposed to hate and kill. After all, they understand each other. They do the same job. In this respect, they resemble the eighteenth century generals who used to lunch together before and after they set to work to eliminate each other.[243]

Corresponding with the increased introspection and authenticity in the genre and, again, as directed by the political, military and social environs of the times, the early 1960s witnessed the rise of numerous German-based scenarios as the genre matured into a Cold War standard.[244] Too, and even more importantly, upon the advent of the Cold War, no geographic location other than Germany — and Berlin above all else — came to hold such symbolic value in addition to its political importance. By mutual acquiescence it emerged as a sort of transitional no mans' land between East and West, an anomalous "neutral ground" remarkably reminiscent to that in Cooper's *The Spy.*

243 Atkins 1984, 200.

244 These included fairly conventional subjects such as the burned-out Berlin operative Alec Leamas in Le Carré's *The Spy Who Came in from the Cold* (1963), subjects far from conventional such as the genetic cloning of Hitler in Levin's *The Boys from Brazil* (1976), amateur Nazi sleuths such as Thomas Levy in Goldman's *Marathon Man* (1974), and seasoned professionals like Bernard Samson in Deighton's *Berlin Game* (1983).

Chapter 6. The Cold War Era — Refinement of the Genre

> "We have to live without sympathy, don't we. That's impossible of course. We act it to one another, all this hardness; but we aren't like that really. I mean...one can't be out in the cold all the time; one has to come in from the cold."
> John Le Carré, *The Spy Who Came in from the Cold*, 1963

The Cold War witnessed a conspicuous transformation in the public perception of espionage. Not only did it serve to elevate the general character of spying in the public mind; but it also made spies even socially acceptable because a more attractive and more highly motivated type of individual appeared to be engaged in espionage.[245] This is probably due in no small part to the number of books that were written during and after the war about the exploits of the Office of Strategic Services, the military forerunner of the CIA, and the adventures of its members. While many of these were written in the guise of autobiography, in reality they read more like fiction. But whatever their literary pretensions, they had the same effect: glamorizing the spy as a romantic hero.

By the early 1960s, espionage fiction, albeit certainly not in all cases, only served to enhance this perception of romance with exotic loca-

---

245 Dulles 1969, iv.

tions, pervasive adventure, intrigue and — in the James Bond frame of reference — abundant opportunity for sexual conquest. But there were also deeper, more complex dynamics at play. During the Cold War, the archetypal spy novel expressed a relatively simplistic view of the world divided between the good — the Western democracies — and the bad — the Soviet Union and its Communist satellite states. It also celebrated man as an individual, with free choice and the ability to change situations. Taken together these two factors were indeed refreshing when cast against an increasingly complex geopolitical world wherein superpowers had adopted such scholarly strategies as mutually assured nuclear destruction to resolve differences. In the absence, then, of major wars, the spy soon emerged as the hero of the post-war world.

As fiction follows fact, the Cold War served to focus the genre toward, if not a completely new reality, surely a new interpretation of the contours of reality as seen through the eyes of authors such as Ian Fleming, Len Deighton and John Le Carré. As Le Carré observes of the era: "We won that war. We squandered the peace. We simply haven't risen to our victory. When we talk about the new enemy, to some extent, it's ourselves."[246]

IAN FLEMING ~

> Women were for recreation. On a job they got in the way and fogged things up with sex and hurt feelings and all the emotional baggage they carried around.
> Ian Fleming, *Casino Royal*, 1954

Ian Fleming (1908-1964) is the creator of James Bond, the fictional British agent 007 who was licensed to kill. But while Fleming served in British Naval Intelligence in World War II, his books ranged far from reality, preferring instead to offer colorful locations, beautiful women, and exciting and inventive adventures. Still, James Bond and Ian Fleming are as intertwined in the public consciousness as are Tarzan and Edgar Rice Burroughs or Mickey Mouse and Walt Disney — popular-culture icons who transcend their status as fictional characters and their creators. The pop-culture phenomenon that is James Bond,

---

246 Le Carré 1993.

however, has become far more famous than his creator, Ian Fleming, whose first-rate escapist fiction is today overshadowed by the films it spawned. More than thirty years after the death of the author, his character is still fighting evil in novels as well as in the longest-running, most financially successful series in the history of motion pictures.[247]

Yet, undoubtedly due to this same widespread popularity, Fleming's Bond fiction is often considered to be markedly less sophisticated than that of Fleming's contemporaries, with Fleming himself largely being taken for granted and thus underestimated. But this is not necessarily the case, for Fleming's contributions to the genre's evolution were significant. To be sure, Fleming was a formulaic writer, indeed, one trapped and ultimately wearied by his own creation, James Bond. Further, the style of his novels was to be overshadowed by that of the subsequent film versions which increasingly slipped over into extremes of parody, self-caricature, gadgetry and thrill seeking. But for all that, Fleming helped establish one of the two dominant modes of the Cold War spy thriller by repackaging and renewing it, and the traditional Buchanesque elements of heroic and patriotic adventure were given new Cold War clothes. Fleming possessed an essential faith in British power and prestige despite the erosion of the British Empire. He was also steeped in the mythology of the British Secret Intelligence Service's supremacy, doubtless derived from his wartime service as personal assistant to the director of naval intelligence.[248]

While Fleming's James Bond unmistakably drew on the traditional clubland heros set down by Le Queux, Buchan and the other early British writers, he modified the genre for the 1950s. From the appearance of *Casino Royale* (1953) until his death in 1964, Fleming produced Bond novels almost yearly and they caught on with both British and American audiences. And although Bond's opinion of women will, of course, today be deemed unacceptable, the Fleming novels offered a world of adventurous fun seemingly just around the corner from the dingy reality of the 1950s. Bond operated on the margins: a safe step just beyond the moral and social conventions of the day.[249]

247 Collins 1998, 367.
248 Wark 1998, 1207.
249 Ibid.

Ian Fleming was born in London to a well-to-do family that believed deeply in service to country. He was educated at Eton and attended Sandhurst military academy, only to resign to study languages at the universities of Munich and Geneva. He took the Foreign Service exam but to no avail and found himself at the age of twenty-three without a career.[250]

At the onset of World War II Fleming joined British Naval Intelligence, eventually rising to the rank of commander. Owing in part to his facility with languages, he became a personal assistant to Admiral John H. Godfrey, the director of Naval Intelligence.[251] Fleming was typical of the intelligence agents of his time, and thus archetypical of Bond, his creation. He came from a family of class, independent wealth, and a history of service. He attended the right schools but did not excel. As his access to the family wealth was somewhat restricted — and he felt unable to live in this shadow — he struck out to develop his own fortunes which, in part, included the writing of a long-considered novel set in the tropics. He decided to base the story on his wartime experiences in Naval Intelligence and set about crafting a thriller about a British secret service agent whose name he found from the author of a book on ornithology — *Birds of the West Indies* by one James Bond. The book, *Casino Royale* (1953), was successful, selling out its initial 4,750-copy British printing. This led Fleming to write another eleven James Bond adventures.[252]

The plot of *Casino Royale* is completely fanciful and escapist.[253] In the novel, a man named Le Chiffre is a mysterious, rootless cosmopolitan who claims to remember nothing from before 1945, when he emerged from Dachau. He is head of a communist-controlled union in Alsace and an agent of the Soviet Union. Immediately after the war, he invested in a chain of *maisons de tolerance* — legal French brothels, but the law is changed and the brothels are outlawed. He loses his investment and a significant amount of Soviet funds. He must now find a way to get the

---

250 Liukkonen 2002.

251 Godfrey would later serve as the model for James Bond's commanding officer, "M."

252 Fleming also wrote one non-Bond novel, the children's classic *Chitty Chitty Bang Bang* (1964), and two collections of short stories.

253 Basau 2001.

money back or SMERSH, the secret police that polices the rest of the Soviet secret police, will kill him. Le Chiffre plans to recoup his losses by gambling in the seaside resort of *Royale-les-Eaux*. British intelligence plans to ruin him by sending their best gambler to defeat him: Agent 007. But the escapism of the book is exceeded by only its obliviousness to the existing real world geopolitical context: Stalin is ruthlessly consolidating his East European power base, the even more merciless Lavrenti Beria is head of the Soviet secret service, and yet the reader is to believe that East and West have nothing better to do than send multinational teams of intelligence agents to watch a card game in an obscure French resort.[254]

Beginning with *Casino Royale*, the Bond series — in concert, perhaps, with *Playboy* magazine — became known as one of the main sources of the 1960-era male fantasy of the good life being defined by a boundless continuum of sexual endeavor and conspicuous consumption. This is particularly evident in *Casino Royale*: 007 drives a Bentley, and when going to dinner together, he and *Casino Royale*'s requisite female — the ever captivating Vesper Lynd — discuss the best champagnes, the correct way to eat caviar and the importance of fine dining. Bond also presents her a very clear explanation of the rules of baccarat so that the reader might learn something of the game and understand the meaning of such phrases as *neuf à la banque*. Still, the absence of reality had little impact on the novel's popularity.

If anything, Fleming crafts his Bond so as to pursue sexual pleasure without complicating and dulling sentiments, without conventional social rituals, and without enervating feelings of guilt and shame. But, at the same time that he makes his hero a direct exponent of these liberated views, Fleming tells us quite another, more subtle, story in image, characterization, and incident. James Bond's inner song of love is "your lips, they may say yes, yes, but there's no, no in your eyes." Indeed, instead of being straightforward, uncomplicated, and full-blooded bed partners, the Bond heroines carry an aura of fatality, perversity, and, in some instances, helplessness. And, much like children of nature who wander a hostile world, they also bring to the stories a wide rage of psycho-sexual perspectives: worldliness (Tiffany Case, Pussy Galore), outdoor-girl self-sufficiency (Honey), international-set glossiness (Tracy), belief in the organization (Tatiana), lesbianism (Pussy Galore), neurosis (Honeychile Rider, a nearly pathological man-hater; Tracy, a nymphomaniac), and treachery (Vesper and Tatiana, enemy agents). Poe pointed out long ago that nothing is quite as exciting as a beautiful dead woman. Fleming, quite clearly, looks to agree, for the mortality rate of Bond heroines is remarkably high.[255]

One of the most frequent criticisms of Fleming's series of James Bond novels is that they are so similar as to be indiscernible from one another, and it is true that there are characters, situations and sequences that are common to and expected of a Bond narrative. A Bond novel is simply not a Bond novel without megalomaniac villains, exotic locations or a heroine with a risqué name. As a result they are predictably cliché with each story line possessing a fixed sequence of "moves" that are orchestrated and constituted according to a perfectly prearranged scheme:[256]

A: "M" moves and gives a task to Bond.
B: Villain moves and appears to Bond (perhaps in vicarious form).
C: Bond moves and gives a first check to Villain or Villain gives first check to Bond.
D: Woman moves and shows herself.
E: Bond takes Woman (possesses her or begins her seduction).
F: Villain captures Bond (with or without Woman, or at different moments).
G: Villain tortures Bond (with or without Woman).
H: Bond beats Villain (kills him, or kills his representative or helps at their killing).
I: Bond, convalescing, enjoys Woman, whom he then loses.[257]

All the moves are apparent in each of Fleming's Bond novels, although each move may appear more than once and they do not always occur in the same sequence. The reader, therefore, finds himself immersed in a game of which he knows the pieces and the rules — and perhaps the outcome — and draws pleasure simply from following the minimal variations by which the victor (Bond) realizes his objective.[258]

---

255 Cawelti and Rosenberg 1987, 144; Amis 1965, 48-49.
256 The novelist Umberto Eco, who is a professor of semiotics and literary criticism at Italy's University of Bologna, is perhaps the leading authority on the structure of Fleming's Bond novels. His conclusions, which I liberally cite here, can scarcely be improved upon.
257 Eco 1979, 156.
258 Ibid., 160.

Doctor No (1958) can thus be termed the archetypal Bond novel as the moves run A-B-C-D-E-F-G-H-I, whereas *Goldfinger* (1959) is structured B-C-D-E-A-C-D-F-G-D-H-E-H-I. By altering the order of the moves, and repeating some and not others, Fleming seemingly endeavors to prevent the books from becoming entirely predictable. Fleming also adds to and changes various secondary elements of the narratives such as the supporting characters, locations, modes of transport, and methods of capture, torture and escape as another means of disguising the similarities between the novels. He enriches the narrative by unforeseen events, without, however, altering the basic scheme.[259]

To further attempt to distinguish the novels from one another, Fleming directs considerable attention to the villains who, at their most basic level, provide an essential role by becoming the instrument that — without Bond's intervention — would seek to upset the world's equilibrium. Although the villains therefore ultimately perform the same role and function in a Bond narrative, they do so through different means and Fleming typically seeks to differentiate them from one another by providing them with grotesque characteristics and idiosyncrasies: *Thunderball*'s (1961) Largo has hands are twice the normal size; *Dr. No* has metal claws for hands; Mr. Big, in *Live and Let Die* (1954), is gray-skinned and has a massive head; and *Moonraker*'s (1956) Hugo Drax has a scarred face, protruding teeth, wild red hair and an ugly demeanor. This basic underlying structure, while altering the surface details in each novel, creates a clever and comfortable montage of *déjà vu* for the Bond fan.[260]

But their formulas and villains aside, Fleming undertook a subtle refinement in the genre with his Bond novels. While generally not directly basing his plots on real world historical events, he sought to posit his stories so as to be able to exploit societal fears drawn from real world scenarios, such as world domination by sinister forces (*Dr. No* and *Moonraker*), destabilization of the world monetary system (*Goldfinger*), the theft of nuclear weapons by terrorists (*Thunderball*), Soviet espionage (*From Russia with Love* (1957)), and biological warfare (*On Her Majesty's Secret Service* (1963). And against these threats, the novels also

259 Ibid., 157.
260 Ibid., 163.

offered a reassuring political message: the Cold War could be lived with, and nothing had changed the essential realities of supremacy. Political power was still exercised by wise British officials and their unbeatable agents who were capable of foiling even the most dastardly of international conspiracies.[261]

The underlying realism that Fleming was able to bring to his stories because of his experience in espionage turned out to be exactly what the public was looking for. He raised the stakes on sex and violence in a postwar society that seemed starved for the sort of grittiness that Fleming brought to his prose. And, although Fleming is not destined to be acknowledged as a great writer, in all probability he will be remembered as a superior storyteller. And whatever his present standing among readers and critics, Ian Fleming accomplished an extraordinary amount in the history of espionage fiction. Almost single-handedly, he revived popular interest in the spy novel, spawning legions of imitations, parodies, and critical and fictional reactions, thus indirectly creating an audience for a number of genre novelists who followed him. Through the immense success of the filmed versions of his books, his character, James Bond, became the best-known fictional personality of his time and Fleming the most famous writer of thrillers since Sir Arthur Conan Doyle.[262]

But, with respect to authenticity, Bond's adventures were ill-suited to the more ominous realities of the Cold War, which were punctuated by tense East-West altercations such as the 1960 downing of an American U-2 spy plane over the Soviet Union, and the Soviet deployment of nuclear missiles in Cuba in 1962. To meet these new realities, there existed another spy novel "modification" waiting in the wings to be rediscovered and reinvented. As Fleming had done with the older, heroic and clubland spy stories, beginning in the early 1960s a very different style of espionage fiction was offered up by two emerging writers — Len Deighton and John Le Carré — who would come to dominate the genre for the next forty years. Both men, like Fleming, also looked back to earlier times, but, in Deighton's and Le Carré's cases, it was to the interwar years and the dark morality of Maugham, Ambler and Greene

---

261 Wark 1998, 1207.
262 Grella 1990, 93.

and their tradition of anti-establishment motifs and revelations of Machiavellian intrigue, duplicity and treachery. Indeed, the 1960s, with its Cold War traumas, Vietnam War, rise of political protest, and growing disenchantment with big government, provided the perfect setting for an "anti-Bond" espionage novel.[263]

LEN DEIGHTON -

> Harvey turned to me and began to relight his cigarette. Americans don't often relight an inch of cigarette so I watched Harvey's lips. He mouthed "O.B.Z." under the cloak of his cupped hands. I didn't nod.
>
> — Len Deighton, *Funeral in Berlin*, 1965

Len Deighton (born 1929) has established himself as one of the major practitioners of spy fiction along with Graham Greene, Eric Ambler and John Le Carré. His novels are praised for their sense of realism and their portrayal of espionage, and Deighton's ability to describe various locations and scenes, qualities partly achieved by Deighton's extensive research and attention to detail. Drawn from actual political events, there is also a considerable level of realism in Deighton's books, particularly in the scenarios involving East-West espionage activities in Cold War Berlin.

Deighton was the first to challenge the Bond formula with his novel *The Ipcress File* (1962). The novel features an unnamed, bemused, but enduring protagonist who operates in a world in which the threats are obscure and the evildoers rather invisible.[264] But more importantly, it is set well apart from the world of earlier writers in that — arguably for the first time — it emphasizes, without significant fuss, a new residency for the mistrust and trickery. While the earlier writers had, of course, been aware of mistrust and trickery, these had been the prerogatives of the enemy, who were cowardly, villainous, and deceitful. But with Deighton — and, of course, his contemporaries — we witness the birth of a new, somewhat grayer world, in which there is absolutely no doubt that British spies have nothing to learn about villainy and

---

263 Wark 1998, 1208
264 The character is later called Harry Palmer and played by Michael Caine in the film adaptation.

disloyalty from their enemies. For, after the Guy Burgess-Donald Maclean spy fiasco there could be no further pretence: defectors came from the top drawer. Indeed, it was a perplexing political time and the spy novel scurried to catch up with life.[265] *The Ipcress File*, for example, opens with the briefing of a cabinet minister on the latest espionage case; the protagonist acknowledges at the outset: "It's a confusing story...I'm in a very confusing business."[266]

The Ipcress File, in fact, revels in confusion and a persistent mockery of Western intelligence and military establishments. The hero, a man at odds with his masters, must puzzle out a plot that involves defecting atomic scientists, brainwashing, and treachery from within. He does so only after suffering confinement and brainwashing himself. He even has an "insurance policy," a little unpatriotic trafficking with the enemy, in case his own untrustworthy chiefs turn on him.[267] In the novel, a number of leading Western scientists have been kidnapped only to reappear a few days later. Unfortunately, each scientist has been brainwashed and is now completely useless. The British send their agent — Deighton's unnamed protagonist — to investigate and, ultimately, he plays a part in the rescue of a biochemist who has been abducted to Lebanon en route to the Soviet Union. While *The Ipcress File* provides a modest glimpse into the uncertainty of the espionage business — while also mocking the spy and military establishments of Britain and the United States — it more importantly sets the tone for the majority of Deighton's subsequent espionage novels with their interrelated and increasingly complex themes of loyalty, betrayal and double agentry.

Len Deighton was educated at the Royal College of Art in London. After leaving school he served in the Royal Air Force and later as the art director of an advertising agency in London, where he began writing *The Ipcress File*. The insouciance of Deighton's anti-establishment spy was an early trademark and signaled a new course for the spy novel, one in which the reader refused to be gulled by tricks and sham certainties, or by a hidden appeal to order and patriotism as was required by the Fleming novels.[268] Too, Deighton brought to the genre dialogue that

265 Atkins 1984, 236.
266 Deighton 1968, 10.
267 Wark 1998, 1208.
268 Ibid.

exhibited a new sharpness and class-consciousness that caused him to emerge as a kind of poet of the spy novel.[269] "Better than Fleming," said some critics, though it must be admitted this was most likely due to their dislike of Fleming rather than their love for Deighton.

The Ipcress File was serialized in the *London Evening Standard* and the film rights were sold soon afterwards. While the book's main character remained nameless, he also had a social anonymity — that of a working-class boy from Burnley in Lancashire — suddenly precipitated into a strange new world of intrigue among people out of his class whom he did not trust. This background gave Deighton's hero an unusual appeal as well as an added feeling of identification and the creation of this slightly anarchic, wise-cracking, working-class hero was Deighton's most original contribution to espionage fiction. When taken together with Deighton's characteristic highly elliptical expositional manner, with his fascination with the technical nuts and bolts of espionage, and with his gift for vivid, startling description, it becomes clear why the first seven of Deighton's spy novels have become genre classics.[270]

Deighton's reputation as an espionage fiction writer was enhanced by *Funeral in Berlin* (1964) — his second "Harry Palmer" story — that detailed an attempt to smuggle a defecting East German biologist out of Berlin. With the help of a high-ranking Russian agent, former Nazi intelligence officers and a freelance agent of doubtful allegiance, Deighton's hero arranges the details of the defection. While the plot has the requisite number of twists and intrigues, this story also illustrates Deighton's fascination with gimmickry through his explanations of technical particulars, such as how to tap a telephone, that were helpfully provided in footnotes. By providing the technical minutiae, Deighton — not unlike his contemporary John Le Carré, who also added similar detail — thought to educate the public about the realities of espionage, in a far more entertaining and subtle way than previously seen.

In Deighton's third "Harry Palmer" novel, *Billion Dollar Brain* (1966), we find that Harry no longer spies for the British and is instead a starving private detective. He receives a package of money, which is followed by a mechanical voice that gives him his instructions over the phone.

---

269 Symons 1993, 249.
270 McCormick and Fletcher 1990, 73.

He accepts the assignment and finds that he has entered the world of a Texas billionaire who is behind an ambitious plot to overthrow Communism with the aid of a super computer. This novel was also brought to the screen, again starring Michael Caine as Harry Palmer.

In later novels, as Deighton matured as a writer, he acquired more sophisticated story-telling techniques and began to rely less upon the gimmickry of espionage. In 1983 he crafted a trilogy, which began with the publication of *Berlin Game* (1983), followed by *Mexico Set* (1984) and *London Match* (1985).[271] These books introduced Bernard Samson, a British intelligence agent. Although older and more cynical than Deighton's earlier "Harry Palmer" character, Samson does share Palmer's disrespect for his superiors and his colleagues who dare to have ambitions.

Berlin Game begins with two agents waiting near the Berlin wall for a defector to cross over from East Berlin. The agent — code-named "Brahms Four" — is the best source the department ever had and the last surviving agent of the Brahms spy network. He wants to get out but fears he will be betrayed by a high-ranking mole in British intelligence. "Brahms Four" will trust only one man — Samson — to come and get him out. So after five years behind a desk in London, Samson is returned to the field, to Berlin, the city where he grew up and the only place where he feels at home. *Berlin Game* is generally considered to be one of Deighton's best books because his grasp of Berlin, his characters and even the smallest details of his narrative are so sharp. It was a book that stripped away the age-withered, custom-staled betrayals of a quarter century of spy novels, perhaps even of history, and once again made painful, real and alive, the true meaning of treason.[272]

In the second novel, *Mexico Set*, the story continues and although Samson has uncovered a spy in British Intelligence — his own wife as it turns out — he allows her to escape; but due to his proximity to the circumstances, his superiors naturally suspect him. To test his loyalty he is sent to Mexico, where he tries to persuade a Russian KGB agent to defect. Attempts to enroll the communist agent take Samson from London to Mexico, Paris and Berlin. In the final novel of the trilogy, *London*

---

271 In 1987 the trilogy, *Game, Set and Match* was made into a 13-part series by Granada Television.
272 Olcott 1990, 73.

Match, the Russian has defected to the British. However, the debriefing is not going well and the Russian insists on talking to Samson, who has to decide whether the Russian is telling the truth when he says that there is another highly placed Soviet mole in British intelligence, or whether the Russian is a plant sent over to discredit Samson himself.

London Match is the most complex novel of the trilogy and perhaps it is the city of Berlin itself that emerges as the best character in the book. It is a living presence and in some of the descriptions one can almost hear the pavement breathing.[273] The *Game, Set, and Match* trilogy is an excellent example of the Cold War's obsession with moles, double agents and the recurrent themes of treachery and betrayal in espionage fiction. The trilogy also reflects the popular interest in Britain at the time with respect to Soviet penetration of British intelligence and, again, details the bureaucratic infighting and turf battles between intelligence agencies and operatives.[274]

Following upon the popularity of the Samson stories in the "*Game, Set and Match*" trilogy, Deighton soon followed up with a second trilogy with Bernard Samson as the central character. The first of these was *Spy Hook* (1988), in which Samson stumbles on financial irregularities within British intelligence that have resulted in the disappearance of millions of pounds. This was followed by *Spy Line* (1989), wherein Samson, after exposing the irregularities in the agency, finds himself branded a traitor with a warrant issued for his arrest. He is forced to abandon his life, his job, his position and plunge into hiding in Berlin. He eventually deduces that the whole affair has been orchestrated by the British intelligence for its own less than honorable purposes. The final book of the second trilogy is *Spy Sinker* (1990); it deals with the enigma of Bernard Samson's wife, Fiona, a beguiling Oxford graduate

---

273 Lester 1990, 74.
274 In 1981, British Prime Minister Margaret Thatcher was forced by the publication of Chapman Pincher's *Their Trade Is Treachery* (1981) to admit that her government had investigated Sir Roger Hollis, the former director general of MI-5, as an alleged Soviet agent. Ms. Thatcher stated in Parliament that a high-level investigation of these charges found them to be false. In the book, Pincher offered a detailed exposition of the case against Hollis and Graham Mitchell, one of Hollis' principal assistants. The book is an excellent example of the "mole mania" that swept through Western intelligence agencies in the late 1970s and early 1980s.

and British agent who has penetrated the East German Stasi at the behest of the KGB in a complex triple agent relationship.

Their popularity now assured, Deighton soon embarked on yet another trilogy involving the venerable Bernard Samson: *Faith* (1994) a post-Cold War story in which Deighton gives his, and Samson's, account of how the Berlin Wall fell and the West prevailed; *Hope* (1995) a post-Cold War story that pits Samson against the new alignments of Eastern Europe; and *Charity* (1996), the final book in the Samson series, in which Samson, who has become increasingly disenchanted by espionage's cultural shifts and political uncertainties, and struggles with a range of family issues while simultaneously maintaining — and expressing — his now predictable indifference to superior officers and agency rules.

But while there is no question that Deighton was instrumental in turning espionage fiction away from the James Bond stereotype and back toward the darker elements of intrigue, duplicity and treachery, the main puzzle about Len Deighton is that, while being such a good writer, he is not even better. One feels he ought to be placed in the same class as Le Carré and Greene but just fails, and if one were making out his school report it would be necessary to state that he could do better.[275] As one critic observed, "While Deighton's laconic style captivates, his impossibly complex plots leave the reader intrigued, but often baffled. Further, there is his recurring theme of betrayal, failure and loss which some readers find utterly depressing."[276]

This said, despite his critics Deighton remains one of the most popular spy novelists, largely due to his attention to detail and his reliance upon real world political and intelligence activities for credible scenarios. His broad appeal is the product of his complete oneness with the environment he describes and in which he lives. In this sense, Deighton emerges as a truly contemporary writer creating, in a sense, his own contemporaneity as he goes along.[277]

---

275 Atkins 1984, 232.
276 Adams 1990, 74.
277 Atkins 1984, 239.

JOHN LE CARRÉ ~

> All power corrupts. The loss of power corrupts even more.
> We can thank an American for that advice. It's quite true. We
> are a corrupt nation, and we need all the help we can get. That is
> lamentable and, I confess, occasionally humiliating. However, I
> would rather fail as a power than survive by impotence. I would
> rather be vanquished than neutral. I would rather be English
> than Swiss.
> — John Le Carré, *A Small Town in Germany*, 1968

A more formidable challenger to the Bond phenomenon was John
Le Carré (born 1931), the pseudonym of David John Moore Cornwell.
In his first three novels — *Call for the Dead* (1961), *A Murder of Quality*
(1962), and *The Spy Who Came in from the Cold* (1963) — Le Carré sets out
the fundamental themes that recur in all of his work. Basic to his novels
are the questions of human values conflicting with pragmatic actions,
as defined by espionage and the moral ambivalence and duplicity of the
intelligence services. Following the critical and commercial success of
The Spy Who Came in from the Cold, Le Carré was encouraged to resign from
his position at the British Foreign Office. But his experience serving in
the front lines of the Cold War in Germany sharply marked *The Spy Who
Came in from the Cold*, and the novel provided the mold for what would
become standard features of the Le Carré espionage story.[278]

David John Moore Cornwell was born in Poole, Dorset, England.
He attended Sherborne School, Berne University and Lincoln College,
Oxford, prior to beginning his career as a tutor at Eton in 1956, teaching French and German. He then joined the Foreign Office, which — he
has recently acknowledged — provided the cover for his intelligence
activities. For five years, 1959 to 1964, he was directly involved in secret
intelligence work. From 1960 to 1963 this was under the guise of second
secretary at the British Embassy in Bonn, and, in 1964, as British consul
in Hamburg.[279]

Le Carré's espionage novels all emerge as commentaries on the
politics of intelligence yet understood in a new way. They are not the
familiar thriller politics of good and evil, white hats and black hats,
us versus them variety; they are instead the politics of power and of

---

278 Beene 1998, 571; Wark 1998, 1209.
279 McCormick 1977, 108.

commerce: archetypal bureaucracies and microcosms of the societies in which they furtively operate. They have hierarchical structures and access to secrets, both of which define power. But the power that resides in intelligence services carries its own mode of corruption, the fact of which Le Carré is singularly mindful.[280]

The Spy Who Came In From the Cold is basically the complex cover-up of a double agent, Hans-Dieter Mundt, who has been planted by British intelligence in the East German Stasi. Mundt, an assassin previously identified by the British intelligence — termed by Le Carré as "Circus" — has been allowed to escape in return for his agreement to spy for the British. Upon returning to East Germany, Mundt soon rises to become a senior official in the Stasi counterintelligence apparatus. Mundt is an anti-Semite, and one of his assistants, an East German Jew named Fiedler, soon suspects Mundt's double agentry and begins to amass evidence of his betrayals.

"Circus" decides that it must mount an operation to protect Mundt not only by eliminating Fiedler, but by removing any grounds for suspicion against Mundt. The plan is to make the East Germans think that the British are mounting a plot against Mundt and that Fiedler is a knowing or unknowing participant in that plot. Thus, when the supposed plot is exposed to the East Germans, Fiedler will be accused either of gross negligence or complicity, and Mundt will be exonerated beyond the slightest doubt.

In order to execute the scheme, "Circus" — through "Control," Le Carré's term for Alec Leamas' supervisor — turns to Leamas, the cynical, burned-out, former head of British intelligence's Berlin station. Telling Leamas that it is a plot to destroy Mundt, "Control" persuades Leamas to pretend to go to seed and become a defector so that he can plant information with the East Germans that will incriminate Mundt as the recipient of large funds from "Circus." "Control" does not tell Leamas that the real object of the operation is not the destruction but the protection of Mundt. Instead, he exploits Leamas' hatred of Mundt, who murdered Leamas' own East German network, to insure Leamas'

---

280 Wark 1998, 1209.

participation in the plot. Because Leamas is only partially in on the plot, "Control" devises another way of exposing the scheme.[281]

Le Carré attracted a serious readership primarily because he provided relief from the unreality and snobbishness of the Bond books and also gave a much more accurate interpretation of the rival secret services during the Cold War period. As a result, his contribution to the genre, and his eventual and unparalleled dominance of it, went well beyond raising the aesthetic qualities of the spy story. Le Carré refashioned the spy novel's apparent realism. In doing so, he was simultaneously turning away from Fleming and building on the work of his predecessors: Buchan had discarded the strident tactic of applying deceptive facts employed by Le Queux and relied instead on topicality as an authenticating device; Maugham had imbued the spy story with a darker morality; Ambler had altered its politics; and Greene had deepened its psychology. Le Carré added to all this by the simple but masterful stroke of inventing for the spy thriller a new vocabulary. His language — of safe houses, watchers, the Circus, the Nursery, babysitters, lamplighters, and so on — invested the familiar with a parallel and more sinister meaning. This language game mirrored the distorting effects that espionage has, in Le Carré's fiction, on everything from public politics to the private love between individuals.[282]

In the end, Leamas, finds himself the unintended victim of the plot and dies on the Berlin Wall in a sacrificial moment in which he chooses not to carry on with the spy game but to join his dead lover, Liz, in the no mans' land of the Berlin Wall itself. The novel is dark in tone, full of anger and passion, and the characterization and plot are skillfully developed. In these ways, *The Spy Who Came in from the Cold* was a direct literary challenge to Fleming, and indeed to Deighton. Moreover, this

---

281 In an intricate series of events, this was effected by Leamas during the period of his pretended decline and upon his entering into a serious love affair with a young woman named Liz Gold. Liz is a Communist party member who can be manipulated into going to East Germany. She is victimized into doing so and becomes an innocent witness at the trial of Mundt. Her testimony proves that in spite of his apparent separation from the service, Leamas is still involved with British intelligence, thus establishing that he is not a confused defector, but an active agent and part of a plot to destroy Mundt. Liz Gold's innocently delivered evidence seals the fate of Fiedler and brings about her own death and that of Leamas.

282 Wark 1998, 1209.

challenge was further expanded by the 1965 film, with Richard Burton playing the role of Leamas, which significantly contributed to Le Carré's reputation as a serious espionage novelist.[283]

As crafted by Le Carré, the figure of Alec Leamas is perhaps one of the most enduring — if tragic — characters in espionage fiction. Leamas is not a contemplative man; on the contrary he is extremely hostile to philosophy of any sort. When his lover asks him what he believes in, he replies, "I don't like Americans and public schools."[284] When his East German interrogator asks him to state his philosophy, Leamas tersely answers, "I just think the whole lot of you are bastards."[285] Leamas later adds: "I don't believe in anything, don't you see — not even destruction or anarchy. I'm sick, sick of killing but I don't see what else [the Secret Service] can do. They don't proselytize; they don't stand in pulpits or on party platforms and tell us to fight for Peace or for God or whatever it is. They're the poor sods who try to keep the preachers from blowing each other sky high."[286]

This rejection of ideology is, of course, directly related to his spying and, in this respect, Leamas believes that philosophies are dangerous because they make people willing to destroy simply for the sake of philosophy. His ultimate justification of secret service, therefore, is that it helps keep the ideologists from destroying the world. Leamas faces the world with hostile suspicion and cynicism. His capacity for love and trust has been almost totally blunted by his lifetime experience of corruption and betrayal, resulting in an inability to feel ordinary human emotions and feelings — a "burnt-out case" so to speak.[287] When, early in the story, his superior wonders if Leamas is tired or burned out, Leamas cynically replies, "That's up to you."[288] Then, with Leamas as the specimen, Le Carré proceeds to educate the reader by providing some measure of insight into the progression of "burning out": "The process of going to seed is generally considered to be a protracted one, but in Leamas this was not the case. In the full view of his colleagues he was

---

283 Ibid.
284 Le Carré 1965, 35.
285 Ibid., 124.
286 Ibid., 215.
287 Cawelti and Rosenberg 1987, 161-162.
288 Le Carré 1965, 18.

transformed from a man honorably put aside to a resentful, drunken, wreck — and all within a few months."[289]

Yet, behind his facade of toughness and moral exhaustion, Leamas desperately wishes to regain his lost sense of human feeling. His hard-boiled attitude is the mask he wears to conceal from others and from himself his true sensitivity to people and events, a sensitivity he has not altogether lost in spite of the horrors and betrayals he has experienced. Still, Leamas' superiors chose to exploit his remaining underlying humanity to further their own operational plans. Leamas, ironically, is aware of his exploitation for professional reasons and is even willing, again for professional reasons, to condone such deceit, despite the personal sense of abhorrence he feels as a result of his espionage activities. For Leamas, the abhorrence seems personified in the form of a recurrent nightmarish memory:[290]

> As he passed the car he saw out of the corner of his eye four children in the back, waving and laughing, and the stupid, frightened face of their father at the wheel. He drove on, cursing, and suddenly it happened; suddenly his hands were shaking feverishly, his face was burning hot, his heart palpitating wildly. He managed to pull off the road into a lay-by, scrambled out of the car and stood, breathing heavily, staring at the hurtling stream of giant lorries. He had a vision of the little car caught among them, pounded and smashed, until there was nothing left, nothing but the frenetic whine of klaxons and the blue lights flashing; and the bodies of the children, torn, like the murdered refugees on the road across the dunes.[291]

This, too, is new ground. Previously, Graham Greene's burnt-out cases are usually defined by their alienation from God, like the drunken priest in *The Power and the Glory*. Their redemption involves a renewal of their faith that, in turn, enables them to act morally in the world. But Le Carré's burnt-out cases are, like Alec Leamas, alienated from their fellow human beings by the dehumanizing forces of twentieth century society. Their redemption is not religious but humanistic and involves a new growth of trust in the ordinary pleasures of life and in friendship

---

289 Ibid., 24.
290 Cawelti and Rosenberg 1987, 163.
291 Le Carré 1965, 106.

and love with others.[292] In this respect, Le Carré proceeds to offer a measure of hope of — and the vehicle for — Leamas' own "redemption" when Leamas considers his relationship with his lover Liz Gold: "He knew then what it was that Liz had given him; the thing that he would have to go back and find if ever he got home to England; it was the caring about little things — the faith in ordinary life; that simplicity that made you break up a bit of bread into a paper bag, walk down to the beach and throw it to the gulls. It was bread for the sea gulls or love, whatever it was he would go back and find it; he would make Liz find it for him."[293]

But in the end this realization comes too late, for Leamas remains trapped in plots and counterplots from which he cannot escape. His death, however, takes on a tragic turn because he has seemingly changed from a clandestine agent to a caring person. Choosing to die at the Berlin Wall rather than continue to live as a pawn in Cold War machinations, Leamas finally identifies himself with the vision of children being destroyed that had so often haunted him:[294] "They seemed to hesitate before firing again; someone shouted an order, and still no one fired. Finally they shot him, two or three shots. He stood glaring around him like a blinded bull in the arena. As he fell, Leamas saw a small car smashed between great lorries, and the children waving cheerfully through the window."[295]

With Leamas, Le Carré successfully sought to portray an accurate observation of Cold War era espionage activities, but through the eyes of a little, even unexceptional man, whom fate has singled out for exploitation. Too, Leamas reflects the conspicuous sense of helplessness an ordinary man might experience when measured against the grander spectacle of East-West relations and the threat of nuclear destruction. It is the variations on these themes — human values conflicting with pragmatic actions, the moral ambivalence and duplicity of intelligence services, the transforming, ennobling power that love can have — that continue to be found in most of Le Carré's later work.[296]

292 Cawelti and Rosenberg 1987, 164.
293 Le Carré 1965, 93.
294 Cawelti and Rosenberg 1987, 167.
295 Le Carré 1965, 93.
296 Beene 1998, 571.

Le Carré continued to explore British and East German espionage activities in *The Looking-Glass War* (1965). This novel begins with the death of a courier who had been sent to Finland, one of the spy centers of Europe, to collect films taken by a commercial pilot who had flown off course while over East Germany. The film suggests that a new type of rocket site is being established and an agent must be infiltrated into East Germany to confirm British suspicions. The agent turns out to be a Polish sailor who has jumped ship in Britain and been placed under surveillance by British intelligence. Following an extended period of observation, he is recruited to infiltrate a missile installation outside of East Berlin and bring back photos of the new rockets. This was followed by *A Small Town In Germany* (1968) that was set in the same town, Bonn, where Le Carré had been posted during his intelligence service. In this novel the second secretary in the British Chancery, Leo Hartling, has disappeared, and the story deals with topical issues, student riots and rising neo-Fascism, with an ambiguous message about what might happen in the near future in Federal Germany.

Le Carré's refinement of the espionage genre continued in a series of three stories that narrated the conflict between George Smiley of the British Secret Service and the enigmatic Karla, head of the espionage division of the Russian Secret Service, known as "Moscow Centre." Smiley, another of Le Carré's more memorable characters is, on the surface, a colorless man, with a flamboyant wife, but he is also perhaps the best spy catcher in the British secret service. The three novels, *Tinker, Tailor, Soldier, Spy* (1974), *The Honourable Schoolboy* (1977), and *Smiley's People* (1980), were published separately. Each novel is an autonomous unit in a larger structure and can be read, understood, and interpreted individually.

In *Tinker, Tailor, Soldier, Spy*, the first of Le Carré's "Karla Trilogy," George Smiley has been retired for about a year when he finds a friend from his old unit in British Intelligence sitting in his living room. He is taken to the home of an advisor to the prime minister on intelligence matters, where he finds evidence that one of the men in the senior ranks of his old agency is a Russian spy. Smiley is asked to find him, but without official access to any agency files, or letting on that anyone is under suspicion. With only a few old friends, his own powers of deduction and secrecy as weapons, Smiley goes back through the records of intelligence operations to try to detect a pattern of failures that could be attributed to the intrigues of a particular agent.

Smiley's battle against Karla continues in *The Honourable Schoolboy*, which is set in Hong Kong, where British Intelligence is investigating a prosperous businessman who seems to be working for the Soviets. The central character is Jerry Westerby, who wants to identify one of Karla's moles who is working inside Communist China and capture him for the West. The trilogy ends with *Smiley's People*, the last confrontation between Smiley and Karla. Smiley decides to force his enemy out into the open so that his only choice is to defect to the West. This operation is conducted unofficially because the British Secret Service, due to political pressure, cannot be involved in an offensive intelligence operation. It becomes instead a personal mission for Smiley and his friends and espionage contacts that he has accumulated over the years. As can be clearly seen, the three novels which make up the Karla trilogy are very much dominated by Le Carré's fascination with the history of British Intelligence in the 1950s and, in particular, the treachery of Kim Philby, which is reflected in his fiction. In each novel Smiley sets out to discover information that will entrap the Soviet master spy, Karla. But somehow this quest appears irrelevant compared to the information that Smiley discovers on the way, in particular his uncovering of the mole in the British Secret Service.[297]

Following the Karla Trilogy, Le Carré continued to explore the boundaries of the genre. In *The Little Drummer Girl* (1983) he turned his attention to the cause of Palestinian liberation. The central character is an American actress in Britain who is persuaded by an Israeli agent to lose her Arab sympathies and spy for them. In 1986, he published *A Perfect Spy*, drawing on his own relations with his domineering father, and in 1989 he released *The Russia House*, a response to the end of Cold War, where a British publisher becomes involved in espionage by a Soviet woman who acts as emissary for a volatile friend.

The fall of the Soviet Union and reunion of Germany left spy fiction adrift and Le Carré turned his attention to the new roles of espionage. *The Secret Pilgrim* (1991) witnesses the return of George Smiley, now a

---

297 McCormick and Fletcher 1990, 65.

mentor to a younger agent; *The Night Manager* (1993) skirts the world of arms dealers and drug lords; *Our Game* (1995) finds two former spies reflecting the new world alignment at the end of Cold War; *The Tailor of Panama* (1996) has as its background the then future of the Panama Canal; *Single & Single* (1999) is a father-and-son story which also deals with a Russian mafia family; and *The Constant Gardener* (2000), Le Carré's 18th novel — and one which was banned in Kenya — that concerns international pharmaceutical intrigues in Africa.[298]

At this stage of his career, John Le Carré has achieved, and perhaps even surpassed, what could be considered to be the art of espionage fiction. A master of metaphor and language and an architect of the tortured soul for over forty years, Le Carré has written about people straining under ideological conflicts, about betrayal in all its forms, and about irreconcilable problems that dispirited individuals confront trying to maintain their humanity in impossible situations.[299]

But there is considerably more to be gleaned from Le Carré's texts than simply metaphor and language. As Le Carré presents it, the basic problem of modern society is the loss of touch with our full human nature and our consequent tendency to engage in meaningless but destructive action or to wallow in contemplation and thought which leads only to more rationalization and justification of the process of dehumanization which engulfs us. Bureaucracy is, in his view, the reification of endless inaction, while, on the other hand, a thoughtless commitment to action can lead only to destruction. The ultimate naive poem is nuclear war, while the final form of sentimentality is total bureaucratization. The spy is a figure of particular fascination to Le Carré

---

298 With respect to censorship, aside from the banning of Le Queux's novel *Guilty Bonds* (1895) in Russia, and the chapter excision in the American edition of Ambler's *Cause for Alarm* (1938), *The Constant Gardner* appears to be the only recent book by an espionage novelist banned by a government agency. In general, governments tend to focus their censorship efforts on former intelligence officers who seek to publish their nonfiction memoirs, and the rationale for a particular book being censored commonly lies in the former employee's contractual obligation not to divulge classified or national security information or, more often, to protect the agency's intelligence sources and methods of collection and analysis. When viewed in the "national security" light, it then stands to reason that the memoirs of a former head of the British Secret Intelligence Service would garner significantly more government scrutiny than those of, say, a former director of Her Majesty's Stationery Office.

299 Beene 1998, 584.

because he is forced to act out this basic modern dilemma in his own individual situation. As a professional secret agent, he is part of an increasingly ineffective bureaucracy; but as an agent in the field, a man out in the cold, he is in a situation where every action is real, a matter of life or death to him. In this sense he is the modern Everyman and the appropriate protagonist of a literary genre especially expressive of the human condition in the latter half of the twentieth century.[300]

The convolutions of conspiracy in the Le Carré novels are elaborate, with the conflict most often including that which exists between the agent and his own government. Le Carré sees democracies as offering freedom without justice, while the enemy's government seems to advocate justice without freedom. All governments, Le Carré implies, are influencing machines pushing us toward personal collapse. In an authoritarian state the victim tends toward catatonia; in a democracy the influencing machine, like so much of our technology, is faulty, and so we flounder. Paranoia is the prevalent atmosphere of a Le Carré novel and Western civilization is depicted as the residue of countless betrayals and discarded ideals, with its governments so jaded that they can only be moved by conspiracy.[301] But is this reality, or simply Le Carré's cynicism seeping to the surface? In the end, it makes little difference either way, for it is what Le Carré himself seemingly believes and indeed ponders in his ruminations on the era of the Cold War:

> The West, it seemed to me, had dishonored every pledge we had made during the Cold War. We continued to protect the strong against the weak. When small nations were butchered, the best we could manage was the tutting of an anxious bystander. (And the British seemed to know better than anyone every reason in the book for doing nothing.) And while we squandered the peace, I felt, we hunted wistfully for a new means of dividing the world for our greater comfort and safety, now that the Communist thing, rather regrettably, had gone away.
>
> I also suspected post-cold-war expansionism on the part of the British secret services, who already were land-grabbing the traditional responsibilities of our publicly accountable police forces in an attempt to preserve and enlarge their empires. As to Prime Minister John Major's vaunted supervision of those services, I didn't believe a word of it, and don't now. My short experience of the secret world had long ago convinced me that

300 Cawelti and Rosenberg 1987, 186.
301 Broyard 1982.

supervision was illusory. The spies weave and duck and cover their traces, which is what people of their calling are paid to do. And their supposed gamekeepers become so enamored of their charges that they turn poacher overnight.[302]

But the fact remains: the commerce of espionage and the Cold War — as it was interpreted by Deighton and Le Carré — is undeniably over. Germany has been reunited and the even the Soviet KGB, as well as its East German counterpart, the Stasi, has passed into history.[303] But despite this passing, the genre of espionage fiction — and, in particular, its reliance on reality-based geopolitical events — continues to evolve as novelists move beyond the Berlin Wall in the search for viable plots and scenarios.

---

302 Le Carré 1995.

303 In 1991, along with the Soviet Union itself, the KGB was dissolved. However, most of its assets and activities have continued through several separate organizations that remain under the Russian military and intelligence umbrella.

CHAPTER 7. BEYOND THE BERLIN WALL — VARIATIONS ON THE THEME

> "No!" the captain cried. "Not if the organization is real and working. Don't you think your colonel knows what he's doing? My God, man, if there's a chance in a hundred of the Reich being restored, how can you not do everything in your power to help make it happen? Think of it, Farnbach! The Reich restored! We could go home again! As heroes! To a Germany of order and discipline in this fucked-up undisciplined world!"
> — Ira Levin, *The Boys from Brazil*, 1976

The most finely crafted of mystery novels and the most formulaic espionage thriller both share the spy story's promise of secrets revealed. Oppenheim, a self-confessed formula writer, well understood the appeal of the spy story: "So long as the world lasts, its secret international history will...suggest the most fascinating of all material for the writing of fiction."[304] Oppenheim's predecessor, Erskine Childers, and even Childers' predecessors Kipling and Cooper, were all aware of the power of secret history at the very birth of the genre. And this secret, often an apocalyptic one, is to the spy thriller what the corpse is to the detective novel. But the secret itself is only part of the spy story; the web of

---

304 Oppenheim 1991, 37.

deception cloaking the secret is what brings the story to life and, to address these factors, one must turn back to conspiracy.

In the spy novel, the narrative must tell how the secret came to be, who controls or competes for it, and what ruin it might bring. In this respect, conspiracy will forever remain wedded to the espionage genre; and conspiracy theory, together with its steady recurrence as a theme in contemporary Western fiction, has reflected the changes within global politics that the world has undergone since the end of the Cold War. By adapting and rearranging its discursive strategies to suit the new political realities arising from national realignments, conspiracy theory has demonstrated its enduring usefulness in a climate of shifting ideological alliances.305 This, in retrospect, is precisely the approach favored by Deighton and Le Carré wherein certain historical facts — the Berlin Wall, nuclear proliferation and the philosophical, as well as geographical, standoff between East and West — provided a viable environment against which to depict their stories. This environment, however, was soon to change.

Official destruction of the Berlin Wall began in June 1990 in the *Bernauer Strasse*. The demolition work was commenced by 300 East German border guards and completed by 600 *Bundeswehr* engineers. The Wall between the two Berlins was completely razed by November 1990, with the exception of six segments kept to commemorate the event. But while destruction of the Berlin Wall held enormous and far-reaching implications for the wider international community, it also wielded tremendous influence on the genre of espionage fiction for, without East and West abutting in Berlin, there could be no more Alec Leamases being shot at the wall; no more Harry Palmers smuggling East German biologists out of Berlin; and, indeed, no anomalous "neutral ground" to be reminiscent of Cooper's *The Spy*.306

---

305 Hantke 1996.

306 On his first official visit to West Germany in May, 1989, Mikhaïl Gorbachev, whose ambition was to save his country from decline and ruin through an innovative policy based on restructuring (perestroïka) and openness (glasnost), informed Chancellor Kohl that the Brezhnev doctrine had been abandoned; Moscow was no longer willing to use force to prevent democratic transformation of its satellite states. This conversation foreshadowed the end of East Germany, for her very existence had no justification apart from ideology.

Would the genre be impacted? With respect to the Le Carré-like interpretations of East-West relations, the answer is an unequivocal yes; however, in another sense, the influence of extrapolative history would become even more prevalent as espionage novelists who, by the 1950s, had already begun to explore other non-Le Carré-like approaches to the post-World War II premise of the genre: the all but limitless intrigues — past, present and future — adapted from documented geopolitical historical activities, or from selected applications of conspiracy history coupled with the popular theme of a resurgent Fourth Reich.

Selected Historical Scenarios -

Although Le Carré-like espionage novels — those concerning moles and rival intelligence services — continue to be written, the formula is more or less tied to a particular world and a particular period. To escape these confines, many spy novelists have taken to threading the margins between fact and fiction when plotting their stories. While historical accounts select, arrange and make value judgments on information, the genre authors either consciously or unconsciously exclude facts that do not support plot development — or color facts so as to support the plot — and then generate carefully crafted narratives that, from the reader's perspective, assume complete authority.

Conversely, from the novelist's perspective — and as obliged by plot and character development factors — the representation of history then becomes the history of representation, with the spy story itself embracing the mantle of something more akin to the pseudo-documentary: a text that is not altogether fiction, but neither is it altogether nonfiction.[307] And, to be sure, this kind of "pseudo-documentary" approach to the genre has certainly not been lost on novelists such as Alistair Maclean with *The Guns of Navarone* (1957); Jack Higgins with *The Eagle has Landed* (1975); and Ken Follett with *Eye of the Needle* (1978), all three of whom have captured mass international audiences with fictional-historical-espionage scenarios.

---

307 Symons 1974, 250.

Alistair Maclean (1922-1972) was born and educated in Glasgow, Scotland. He served in the Royal Navy during World War II and following the war taught at Glasgow University until 1955, when he became a full-time writer. Maclean wrote nearly thirty espionage and adventure novels, most of which follow historical themes. Usually MacLean's heroes are calm, cynical men who carry some kind of secret knowledge. They fight against incredible odds and, of course, there are the evil opponents, a wide variety of humorless villains, the Nazis, terrorists, Communists, drug dealers and foreign agents. During the course of the story, the protagonist is pushed to the limits of his physical and sometimes mental endurance. Nature is a central element in MacLean's work, especially North Atlantic Seas, mountains, desert quick sands, and frozen Arctic tundra. Maclean is perhaps best known for his novel *The Guns of Navarone*, which typifies the application of the historical espionage-adventure story as set against the backdrop of World War II.

In *The Guns of Navarone*, twelve hundred British soldiers are stranded on the island off the Turkish coast and could be rescued if the Nazi gun emplacement at Navarone could be put out of action. Two large artillery pieces guard the Aegean waters between Greece and Turkey — through which the British evacuation convoy must pass — and conventional means of destroying the emplacement, by both naval and land assaults, have failed. A clandestine operation is planned that involves a multinational team of five Allied specialists who must scale impossible cliffs, avoid German patrols, and ultimately sabotage the Nazi artillery. They have just under three days and four nights to execute this impossible mission and, unbeknownst to the others on the team, a traitor lurks in their midst.

Jack Higgins — the *nom de plume* for Harry Patterson (born 1929) — also turned to World War II for the backdrop to his 1975 espionage novel *The Eagle has Landed*, which has become a classic example of the documentary-style approach to fiction. Higgins was brought up in Belfast in a family with a political background. He held a succession of jobs, including two years as a noncommissioned officer in the British Royal House Guards, serving on the East German border during the Cold War. He was then accepted as an external student at London

University and eventually gained a degree in sociology and social psychology and went into teaching before becoming a full time author.

The Eagle has Landed is set in 1943 and involves a Nazi plot by Heinrich Himmler to send a small group of commandos to kidnap Churchill from the safety of the English countryside and spirit him back to Germany. For the Nazis, it would be a considerable propaganda victory; additionally, it would be exactly the sort of high-risk operation that would appeal to Hitler, thereby giving Himmler a measure of one-upmanship over the regular German military. The plan seems unworkable until serendipity intervenes: Joanna Grey, a South African-born Nazi agent in a small village on the coast of Norfolk, reports that the prime minister is planning a weekend retreat in a local manor house. A group of German paratroopers could be flown to the village and then picked up by boat after completing their mission.[308]

Higgins includes a colorful cast of characters to accomplish the mission: the mission commander, Colonel Steiner, who speaks perfect English courtesy of an American mother and is motivated to do Himmler's bidding by the arrest of his Prussian father by the Gestapo; and Devlin, an IRA assassin who is intrigued by the project. Higgins provides his characters with just enough psychological complexity to add depth to the plot, and perceptively depicts the dynamics of life in a small, isolated English village, where everyone is generally aware of everyone else's business.

In *The Eagle has Landed* Higgins employs a unique and extremely effective device to lend his story additional historical credibility: He bookends the main action with a short account about how he himself stumbled onto the story in the 1970s, eventually learning "the truth" in bits and pieces from dozens of interviews with the participants. Because numerous documented, extraordinary plots — many of them inspired by the craftiness of Churchill himself — actually were carried out in prosecution of the war's espionage efforts, Higgins' device serves to add additional credibility to the fictional scenario.

---

308 *The Eagle has Landed* also serves to illustrate the marked difference between the "hero" stereotypes seen in much of the World War II-themed genre fiction, and the more complex characterizations of Le Carré.

Ken Follett (born 1947) also exploited the tapestry of World War II in his 1978 novel *Eye of the Needle*. It is historical fact that, in 1944, the Allies, having recaptured North Africa and battled their way up the spine of Italy, were planning a major cross-English Channel offensive. However, perhaps the most closely guarded secret of the war was the exact site of the landing. The Allied goal was to deceive the Germans into preparing for an invasion of France via the Pas de Calais, then surprise them at Normandy. With the outcome of the war possibly in the balance, the Allies' key prospect for defeating Hitler hinged on the immediate identification and elimination of any German spies in England capable of discovering the elaborate ploy. Set in this time period, one of these German spies was Follett's fictional character Henry Faber, also known as *Die Nadel* — "The Needle."

Follett was born in Cardiff, Wales, and attended University College London, where he studied philosophy. Graduating in 1970, he obtained placement in a graduate journalism course run by Thompson Regional Newspapers, and worked on the staff of the *Evening News*, where he wrote a regular column about the River Thames. Bored with the newspaper business, he began to take up fiction writing in his free time.

For background to *Eye of the Needle*, Follett relied on various nonfiction texts concerning intelligence and espionage activities in World War II. One book in particular was Anthony Cave Brown's critically acclaimed *Bodyguard of Lies* (1975), which described the many ways the Allies deceived and undermined Hitler and detailed how they spied on and employed intelligence and counterintelligence against the Nazis in laying the groundwork for the crucial invasion of Europe. In Brown's book, there was an account of an elaborate deception for the D-Day Invasion wherein the Allies created an entire illusionary army in East Anglia, including inflatable tanks, cardboard Spitfires and barracks with roofs but no walls. The ruse was created to be photographed from the air by German reconnaissance planes so as to deceive the Nazi hierarchy into thinking that the army was building up in the east, indicating that the invasion would come across the narrow part of the channel at Calais. Follett seized upon this scenario and ventured the premise that "what if" *one* German spy had seen the inflatable tanks, the cardboard Spitfires and the whole mock-up from the ground and escaped back to

Germany with the information — the Germans then could have been prepared for the D-Day landings at Normandy and history might have taken a different course of events.

Follett's German spy is code-named "The Needle" because of the stiletto knife he carries up his sleeve to kill anyone who threatens his mission. Scotland Yard Investigator Bloggs and Professor Godliman, recruited from academia into the war effort, pick up the trail of this spy through a timely clue: his habitual use of the stiletto links two murders and ultimately leads to his identification. As the pursuit begins, "The Needle" obtains the crucial information and makes a desperate dash for Germany with Bloggs and Godliman in hot pursuit. As the British authorities close off his avenues of escape, and with time running out before the scheduled invasion, Faber's attempt to flee lands him on a desolate island off Scotland's coast. There, Lucy Rose, a young English housewife, is coping with her wheelchair-bound husband's bitterness over the accident that took his legs and excluded him from the war effort, and with her own loneliness and isolation. Drawn to the stranger until she discovers who he truly is, Lucy must summon the requisite courage and resourcefulness to protect herself, her young son, and England from "The Needle" and to thwart his escape back to Germany by U-boat.

As witnessed by the collective successes of Maclean, Higgins and Follett, the concept of taking historical events and converting selected facts to create a pseudo-documentary atmosphere in which to situate their stories has considerable appeal. But this approach, however attractive, also may become self-restraining, as it requires the writer to place his story within known and established timelines and to employ known and accepted historical accounts. An example of this time-fact constraint emerges with the examination of Henry Faber, the German spy in Follett's *The Eye of the Needle*. To cast Faber waiting for extraction by a Nazi U-boat during the Korean War, for instance, would be seen as implausible. As written, there is only one place in history — England — at one point in time — prior to the Normandy invasion — that Follett's plot would appear credible. As Follett notes, "Thrillers are fantasies. Such authenticity as they may have is designed to distract the reader's attention from the implausibility of the story."[309] And one does indeed suspect that someone like Faber could have existed; but, again, only at that particular time and place in history.

To escape the time-fact constraints of the pseudo-documentary, there emerged another school of post-Cold War genre authors who — similar to Maclean, Higgins and Follett — began with elaborately documented, German-themed historical narratives; but they elected to course their stories away from historical reality in favor of selected counterfactual premises. This direction seems to align itself more closely with the Oppenheim notion of "secret history," for central to the formula are the various Fourth Reich scenarios as typified by Frederick Forsyth's *The Odessa File* (1972); Greg Iles' *Spandau Phoenix* (1993); and Robert Ludlum's *The Apocalypse Watch* (1995), among numerous others.

Selected Resurgent Fourth Reich Scenarios -

As previously indicated, the circumstances of Nazi Germany offers surprising flexibility with respect to the development of fictional plots based upon certain aspects of the Nazi state and its attendant conspiratorial underpinnings. To this end, *The Odessa File*, by Frederick Forsyth, emerges as perhaps the archetypal Fourth Reich scenario. Set in the early 1960s, it is the story of the hunt by a Hamburg newspaperman, Peter Miller, for SS killers living under false identities produced by the ODESSA — a clandestine organization for former members of Hitler's SS.[310]

Frederick Forsyth was born in Ashford, Kent, England in 1938. He was educated at Tonbridge School and later Granada University, Spain. After serving as one of the youngest pilots in the Royal Air Force, at the age of nineteen, Forsyth wrote for the *Eastern Daily Press* in Norfolk before becoming a correspondent for Reuters, then a radio and television reporter for the BBC. As assistant diplomatic correspondent, he covered the Biafran side of the 1967 Biafra-Nigeria war and this provided

---

309 Follett 1990, 96.
310 ODESSA is a word composed of six letters, which in German stand for *Organisation der ehemaligen SS-Angehörigen.* In English this means "Organization of Former Members of the SS." The Nazi SS was the army within an army, devised by Adolf Hitler and commanded by Heinrich Himmler, charged with completing special pogrom activities.

him with the knowledge of international politics and of mercenary soldiers that led him to write *The Day of the Jackal* (1971), which became an
instant success and spawned his writing career.

The Odessa File begins with reporter Miller covering the suicide of
an elderly German Jew who had survived the German concentration
camps in World War II. Through contacts in the local police Miller
obtains the dead man's diary: a cache of documents known as *The Odessa
File* that protects the identities and advances the destinies of former
members of Hitler's SS since shortly before the end of World War II.
ODESSA resembles a Mafia-like organization and is headed by a former
SS Captain Eduard Roschman — known as the "Butcher of Riga" —
who has eluded the various tribunals and other judiciary apparatuses
established after the war. The primary purpose of ODESSA is a ruthless
plot to reestablish the worldwide power of SS mass murderers and to
carry out Hitler's "Final Solution."

In the course of his investigation, Miller is introduced to a world
of Nazi revanchists, Israeli Mossad infiltrators, obstructionist German
bureaucrats and famed Nazi hunter Simon Wiesenthal. But while the
story is indeed fiction, many of the scenarios and questions presented
by Forsyth are based upon real events which provide the novel's historical foundations: What really happened to the German-designed
rockets that Nasser was supposed to have ready in time for the Six
Day War? How did the SS acquire new identities for its members so
quickly after the war's end and where did it get the money needed to
do so? Could the head of a major multinational business organization
be a former officer of the SS and a wanted war criminal? *The Odessa File*
became Forsyth's second international bestseller, and in 1974 the film
version was released with Jon Voight playing the reporter Peter Miller
opposite Maximilian Schell as SS Captain Eduard Roschman.

In *Spandau Phoenix*, Greg Iles (born 1961) seeks to explore the mystery of Hitler's Deputy Fuhrer Rudolph Hess, who was captured after
his inexplicable flight to England at the beginning of the war. Iles, born
in Germany, spent his youth in Natchez, Mississippi and graduated
from the University of Mississippi. *Spandau Phoenix* was his first novel
and it was quickly included on the *New York Times* best sellers list. In
the novel, Iles proposes that Hess' reason for traveling to England was

to seek a separate peace through negotiations with sympathetic British aristocrats. However after his capture and suicide — or was it assassination? — in Spandau Prison, old questions surfaced with respect to his identity: Was this indeed Hess, or was it an imposter? There has always been doubt about his identity and the Russians had always been strangely adamant about paroling the elderly fascist. Then, as Spandau is being razed, a German policeman finds a hidden sheaf of papers that will address this question and, more to Iles' fictional premise, that will also, because of the embarrassing wartime information regarding their own respective countries, prompt a slate of intelligence agencies — Soviet, East German, British, Israeli and American among others — attempt to obtain the documents prior to their public release.

Robert Ludlum's *Apocalypse Watch* introduced the Fourth Reich as the "Brotherhood of the Watch," an ominous neo-Nazi cabal that operates from a remote, fortress-like nerve center in Austria's Hausruck Mountains. Began in the days after the Third Reich's defeat, the Brotherhood is penetrated by a covert CIA operative who ultimately recovers a list of the Brotherhood's secret supporters: various neo-Nazis who are also high-ranking officials in the United States and its allied governments.

Robert Ludlum (1927-2001) was educated at various schools in Connecticut and at Wesleyan University, from which he graduated in 1951. During World War II, he served in the United States Marine Corps and, following the war, he worked as a stage and television actor and as a producer of plays until turning to freelance writing. He published *The Scarlatti Inheritance* in 1971, the first of nearly two-dozen best-selling novels, the vast majority of which were based upon various espionage and intelligence activities themes.

Ludlum possessed a certain fascination with Nazism, and this interest — both in pseudo-documentary, as well as Fourth Reich scenarios — is readily apparent. For example, in *The Rhinemann Exchange* (1974), the backdrop is World War II and the Third Reich is short of industrial diamonds required to build V-2 rockets; however, the United States needs better gyroscopes to make a new bombsight work properly. Dishonest industrialists from the two sides work out a diamonds-for-gyroscope design exchange arrangement. In *The Holcroft Covenant* (1978),

Ludlum deals with a Fourth Reich scenario: In 1945 the children of the Third Reich were secretly hidden all over the world, to be concealed until the 1970s when they would come of age. Then the most elaborate plans and $780 million in a Swiss bank would be waiting to establish them as the new Reich. In 1985, *The Holcroft Covenant* was made into a film starring Michael Caine as Noel Holcroft. Although Ludlum became a major figure in expanding the mass-market popularity of post-Cold War espionage fiction, his work is often criticized and is generally considered to be something less than literature, prompting one critic to observe that despite Ludlum's enormous commercial success, by the late 1990s few if any authors had intentionally or unintentionally tried to emulate him.[311]

Of all the "Fourth Reich rising" circumstances, perhaps none are as creative as those that rely upon interpretation of the various conspiracy theories surrounding Hitler's death in Berlin. From the remotely possible to the patently implausible, even to science fiction, together they form a special category of the Fourth Reich novel: that concerning the numerous "what if Hitler lived" scenarios.

The *Trial of Adolf Hitler* (1978) by Philippe Van Rjndt, for example, proposes that Hitler survived the war and has remained in hiding for years, quietly building the foundation for the Fourth Reich, and that he ultimately appears before the world, stands trial and is acquitted of his crimes. George Steiner's *The Portage to San Cristobal of A.H.* (1982) follows a similar line in that Israeli Nazi hunters find Hitler in the Amazon jungle thirty years after the end of the World War II. After he is captured, he defends himself for his crimes. *The Seventh Secret* (1986) by Irving Wallace is also based on the premise that Hitler survived the war and that an active Nazi movement is still in existence today. *Fatherland* (1994) by Robert Harris proposes that Germany won World War II, Europe is dominated by the victorious German Reich, and that celebrations are underway for Hitler's 75th birthday.

Finally, David Charnay's *Operation Lucifer: The Chase, Capture and Trial of Adolf Hitler* (2001) not only offers an accurate portrayal of the Nazi era during World War II but also a thoroughly drawn scenario as to what might have or should have happened had Hitler survived the war. It fol-

---

311 Goodman 1998, 612.

lows through with the actual chase, capture and trial of the infamous Fuhrer. But even if Hitler indeed died in 1945, his progeny — and presumably his malevolence — could continue to prosper indefinitely, as suggested in Ira Levin's *The Boys from Brazil*, which — due to the film adaptation — is perhaps the best known of the Hitler conspiracy novels.

While *The Boys from Brazil* also relied on historical premise, it sought — at the time of its 1976 publication — to push the genre into an area quite close to science fiction: the genetic cloning of Hitler. Ira Levin is a professional writer and the author of a number of best selling novels including *Rosemary's Baby* (1967) and *The Stepford Wives* (1972). In *The Boys from Brazil* Levin turns his attention to a Fourth Reich scenario, but with a historical premise that is based upon scientific conjecture drawn from extrapolations concerning environment and heredity.

In Levin's story, Joseph Mengele, the notorious Nazi doctor, is discovered to be alive in the Brazilian jungle, where he is manufacturing clones of Adolf Hitler. Each of these is to be adopted by a family as close as possible to Hitler's own — which, among other things, necessitates engineering the deaths of 94 male civil servants as close as possible to their 65th birthday. The murders are an effort to insure that the boy-clones experience the same home environment as *Der Fuhrer* — thus enhancing any genetic determination — and the assassins are six former SS agents who are dispatched from South America by Mengele. Aging Jewish Nazi-hunter Yakov Lieberman slowly uncovers the plot, discovers the truth and moves to thwart Mengele's plan. In the 1978 film adaptation of *The Boys from Brazil*, Gregory Peck played Mengele, while Sir Lawrence Olivier portrayed Lieberman.

But while *The Boys from Brazil*, at least that the time of its release, pushed the boundaries science fiction, *The Proteus Operation* (1996) by James Patrick Hogan embraced it with abandon. In the novel, Hogan combines alternate conspiracy history and hard science fiction, not only proposing that the Nazis had won World War II, but detailing a plot wherein a team of scientists, soldiers and other specialists go back to 1939 to change the course of history. Consequently, when cast against selective applications of genetics and time travel it may well be that the specter of a resurgent Fourth Reich — and even of Adolf Hitler himself — will prosper well into the twenty first century

But the popularity of Ludlum, Follett and the others aside, there have been many who have prophesied the doom of the spy novel, predicting that its prospects are exhausted and that after the varied talents of Fleming, Le Carré and Deighton it is difficult to see how the genre can continue to flourish.[312] And, in some respects, this is possibly true. Since the end of the Cold War, there have been any number of reasons as to why the spy novel might be on its way out; however, most of the rationale is generally related to the fact that there is no longer the same great East and West confrontation.

But even with the fall of the Berlin Wall and the realignment of international coalitions, it is unlikely that either East or West, in the real geopolitical world, will ever regard each other with anything other than a cautious, if benevolent, suspicion. To this end, it then falls to the spy novelist to provide persuasive and illuminating narratives that adapt global historical and political events and processes in search of stories that will continue to give the espionage story its future power, range, and importance. In the final analysis, if three people look at a star in the sky, one will see God, another science and the third conspiracy. And when viewed from this perspective, the spy novel seems destined to endure.

---

312 Denning 1987, 153.

Conclusion

> Beneath the broad tide of human history there flow the
> stealthy undercurrents of the secret societies, which frequently
> determine in the depths the changes that take place upon the
> surface.
> — Arthur Edward Waite, *The Real History of the Rosicrucians*, 1977

Since the 1903 publication of Erskine Childers' *Riddle of the Sands* and
continuing through the work of John Le Carré to today, espionage fiction has witnessed a continual refinement of both tone and complexity
as it reflects society's concerns and anxieties. With Le Queux, Oppenheim and Buchan — and as re-invented by Fleming — plots consisted
of colorful, imaginative adventures with roving, honorable heroes,
dastardly villains and exotic settings. In contrast, the plots identified
with Maugham, Conrad, Ambler, Greene and Le Carré, contain tales of
espionage more realistically presented and more concerned with corruption, betrayal and conspiracy. These stories feature a grayer mood,
more circumscribed settings and ordinary protagonists who seem, at
first glance, not much different than the people they oppose.[313] The
plotting is complicated and subtle, and the endings are often down-
beat, leaving the agent sadly disillusioned or dead. The chief difference
between the two approaches is the moral base of the narrative. With

---

313 Walker 2006.

the earlier authors, good and evil is rendered in stark black and white, while, with their successors, the morality is ambiguous.

Commencing during the Cold War and increasing in frequency after the fall of the Berlin Wall, one begins to observe two additional, distinct — if parallel — transitions in the genre. The first is typified by the works of Maclean, Higgins and Follett, in which there arises a certain reliance on historical fact in the guise of the pseudo-documentary novel. The second transition is that exhibited by genre authors such as Forsyth, Levin and Ludlum who generally begin with a pseudo-documentary slant, yet move toward counterfactual premises that are themselves augmented by selective applications of conspiracy theory. Still, regardless of the approach, most spy novels written since the end of the Cold War have more than kept pace with the contemporary understanding of the profession of espionage, and it is this "understanding" that will perhaps most influence the future of the genre.

As foreshadowed by Conrad and Maugham — and as refined by Deighton and Le Carré — there exists general public discernment that the commerce of espionage is not as simple as it once was and, even more germane, that the political world — similar to their depiction of morality — is no longer delineated by black and white but rather by lesser shades of gray. Good guys and bad are no longer recognizable by the hats they wear, and the governments they represent are equally ambiguous and, thus, at least suspect.[314]

Treason or incompetence in high government circles is, after all, no more than we read about in our newspapers, where we have seen any number of officials in high places exposed as agents for a foreign power. These betrayals, be they personal or political, have been central to achieving the prevailing measure of cynicism about loyalties of any kind to people or to institutions. This, in turn, can be coupled with the suspicion that governments routinely lie to protect and perhaps further their own end, along with the suggestion that influential components of government may well owe their chief allegiance to private corporations or other interest groups. This civic cynicism about issues and leaders finds an outlet in reading about traitors in high places in the spy novel. Times of stress foster paranoia. In our times, the secret agent, caught

---

314 Cawelti and Rosenberg 1987, 188.

in his own crisis of belief, becomes a projection of our own doubts and the highly placed traitor, while not exactly commonplace in the news, is heard of with sufficient frequency to be believable in fiction.

But the appeal of espionage fiction seemingly transcends the political strategies it narrates, which can range from the flamboyant terrorism of the assassin to the clandestine schemes of Fourth Reich conspirators. Its allure is based on the fact that it is a cover story for a culture, and in this lies the success and failure of the spy novel, its utopia and its ideology.[315] Indeed, this is the central attraction of espionage fiction: It serves as a way of narrating individual political activity — that of the spy — in a world of institutions and states that seem to block all individual action. It is seen as a type of game, albeit a valid geopolitical one, in which the anxieties of a particular state, in a particular time — the Oppenheim-Le Queux era comes to mind — can be invested with a sense of measured optimism through the knowledge that somewhere an anonymous spy is acquiring intelligence that can be used to defeat the same particular state's enemy. Brought forward to the Cold War era, a similar scenario exists: Although the world may be skirting the cusp of nuclear annihilation, one may find some degree of reassurance in the knowledge that there are individuals like Le Carré's Leamas who are prepared to die in order to preserve the status quo.

The evolution of espionage fiction is also the evolution of a culture; for, as the genre evolved, so too did Western society. But while there were numerous variations on the theme, the fundamental thread that connects the world of James Fenimore Cooper's 1821 *The Spy* to John Le Carré's 1966 *The Spy Who Came in from the Cold* is the reliance upon the historical reality of their respective eras. For Cooper it was in the guise of the American Revolution; for Le Carré in the clandestine affairs of the Cold War. And although the influence of the historical record was either marginalized or emphasized as dictated by fictional requirements, it nonetheless marks a unique engagement — a historical prism, so to speak — through which to view the genre's evolution.

Following the 1903 publication of *Riddle of the Sands* — and resultant of the empire-building tension of the late nineteenth century — fictional plots in the years prior to World War I witnessed a marked

---

315 Denning 1987, 152.

reliance on Britain's diminishing international status. Oppenheim's *The Maker of History* (1905) and *The Great Secret* (1907) both draw attention to foreign militarism and fuel the growing apprehension of foreign threats to British sovereignty. Le Queux soon joined the trend with *The Invasion of 1910* (1906), *Spies of the Kaiser* (1909), *The Mystery of the Green Ray* (1915), *Number 70 Berlin* (1916), and *The Zeppelin Destroyer* (1916), all of which posited secret foreign spy networks in Britain.

As the genre began to mature, witnessed principally by Conrad's *The Secret Agent* (1907) and *Under Western Eyes* (1911), and Chesterton's *The Man Who Was Thursday* (1908), there was a brief shift away from foreign invasion scenarios in favor of more modest themes such as terrorism and anarchy. However, by 1919, Buchan signaled a return to the foreign invasion premise with publication of *The Thirty-Nine Steps*, a theme he continued with *Greenmantle* (1916), and *Mr. Standfast* (1919).

The years between World War I and World War II saw not only the repositioning of world political order but also a corresponding realignment of espionage fiction. Spurred primarily by Maugham's personal experience in the intelligence service and his publication of *Ashenden: or the British Agent* (1928), there was a turn toward realism and away from the clubland heroes of Buchan's era. The search for realism was continued by Ambler, who concurrently — and with an eye toward world events — reflected the rise of National Socialism and Fascism during the interwar years with *Epitaph for a Spy* (1938), *Cause for Alarm* (1939) and *Journey into Fear* (1940). Greene continued the theme with *Ministry of Fear* (1943) — which was released during the war — that premised a German espionage network operating in Britain.

The end of World War II and the onset of the Cold War again witnessed the repositioning of world political order and, once again, a significant corresponding effect on the evolution of espionage fiction. Prevalent themes centered on the West's sense of isolation as reflected in the new reality of East-West conflagration and the international Cold War of the 1950s and early 1960s. This formula depicts more complex agent characters who find themselves struggling as much with their personal demons as with the omnipresent Soviet threat. While Fleming, in his James Bond novels, sought a return to the clubland hero, his contemporaries Deighton and Le Carré embraced existing geopolitical alignments in numerous Cold War scenarios. Deighton, with *Funeral in Berlin* (1964) and *Berlin Game* (1983), and Le Carré with *The Spy Who Came in from the Cold* (1966), *The Looking-Glass War* (1965) and *A Small Town In Germany* (1968), both viewed the estrangement between East and West Germany — and Berlin in particular — as the twentieth century representation of Cooper's 1821 "neutral ground," and set their stories astride the ambiguity and duplicity that came to mark Cold War espionage activities.

Following the Cold War, the historical record began to encourage the genre's evolution, albeit in two seemingly diverse directions. In novels such as Maclean's *The Guns of Navarone* (1957), Higgins' *The Eagle has Landed* (1975) and Follett's *Eye of the Needle* (1978), we find examples of various espionage plots based upon the World War II historical record. In a second approach, we find evidence of selected modification of the historical record more in line with Oppenheim's notion of "secret histories" — the conspiracy formulas and Fourth Reich scenarios typified by Forsyth's *The Odessa File* (1972), Levin's *The Boys from Brazil* (1976) and Ludlum's *The Apocalypse Watch* (1995).

In the nearly two hundred years since Cooper published *The Spy: A Tale of Neutral Ground*, espionage fiction has without fail sought to reflect the political perceptions of its own particular era. From the journalism of Childers, through the stridency of Le Queux and the topicality of Buchan, and from the moral ambiguity of Ambler through the psychological complexity of Le Carré, the genre has prospered, connected by a perpetual thread that has consistently permeated — and indeed defined — its evolution: the marked engagement with geopolitics and the seamless extrapolation of the historical record.

As Kim Philby stated: "To betray, you must first belong. I never belonged. I have followed exactly the same line the whole of my adult life. The fight against fascism and the fight against imperialism were, fundamentally, the same fight."[316] In this most succinct of statements, we find the seed, the realism, and even the very culture of espionage. For the spy novelist, Philby provides no small measure of insight for he suggests not only where the spy might have been, but why he went there.

---

316 Knightly 1987, 271.

And this, ultimately, is what the spy story is all about. For without the politics, the wars, and the espionage, there could be no fiction to fathom its depth.

Works Cited

Adams, Charles Hansford. *The Guardian of the Law: Authority and Identity in James Fenimore Cooper.* University Park: Pennsylvania State University Press, 1990.

Adams, James. In Donald McCormick and Katy Fletcher, *Spy Fiction: A Connoisseur's Guide.* New York: Facts On File, 1990.

Ambler, Eric. "Afterword." *Epitaph for a Spy.* London: Hodder and Stoughton. 1938.

_____ . "Introduction." *Intrigue: Three Famous Novels in One Volume.* London: Hodder and Stoughton, 1965.

_____. In Donald McCormick, *Who's Who in Spy Fiction.* New York: Taplinger, 1977.

_____. "Still Writing After All These Years." *The Progressive* 59, March: 41.1995.

_____. *A Coffin for Dimitrios.* New York: Carroll & Graf, 1996.

_____. In David Stafford, *The Silent Game: The Real World of Imaginary Spies.* Toronto: Lester and Orphen Dennys, 1998.

Amis, Kingsley. *The James Bond Dossier.* New York: New American Library, 1965.

Andreas, Osborn. *Joseph Conrad: A Study in Non-Conformity*. New York: Philosophical Library, 1959.

Atkins, John. *The British Spy Novel: Styles in Treachery*. London: John Calder, 1984.

Bancroft, William Wallace. *Joseph Conrad, His Philosophy of Life*. New York: Haskell House, 1964.

Basau, Amit K. 2001. "*Casino Royale*, Ian Fleming." *Mystery Guide*. www.mysteryguide.com.

Beene, Lynndianne. "John Le Carré." In Robin W. Winks, ed., *Mystery and Suspense Writers*. New York: Charles Scribner's Sons, 1998.

Benvenuti, Stefano, and Gianni Rizzoni. *The Whodunit: An Informal History of Detective Fiction*. Trans. by Anthony Eyre, with "A Report on the Current Scene" by Edward D. Hoch. New York: Macmillan, 1982.

Bernstein, Stephen. "Politics, Modernity, and Domesticity: The Gothicism of Conrad's the Secret Agent." *CLIO* 32 (3: 285) 2003.

Blanch, Michael. "Imperialism, Nationalism, and Organized Youth." In *Working Class Culture*. London: Hutchinson, 1979.

Borkin, Joseph. *The Crime and Punishment of I.G. Farben*. New York: The Free Press, 1978.

Boucher, Anthony. "Trojan Horse Opera." In Howard Haycraft, ed., *The Art of the Mystery Story*. New York: Simon & Schuster, 1946.

Boyd, Ian. *The Novels of G.K. Chesterton: A Study in Art and Propaganda*. New York: Barnes and Noble, 1975.

Boyle, Andrew. *The Fourth Man*. New York: Dial Press, 1979.

Broyard, Anatole. "Le Carré's People." *The New York Times*, August 1982. http://www.nytimes.com/books/99/03/21/specials/lecarre-people.html

Buchan, John. *The Thirty-Nine Steps*. New York: Dover, 1994.

Cawelti, John G. and Bruce A. Rosenberg. *The Spy Story*. Chicago: University of Chicago Press, 1987.

Chesterton, G.K. "A Defence of Detective Stories." In *The Defendant*. London: J.M. Dent and Sons, Ltd., 1901. http://www.chesterton.org/gkc/murderer/defence_d_stories.htm.

Chesterton. G.K. *The Man Who Was Thursday*. Harmondsworth: Penguin Books, 1986.

Cienciala, Anna M. *The Rise and Fall of Communist Nations, 1917-1997*. Lawrence: The University of Kansas, 2001. http://www.ukans.edu/kansas/Cienciala/342.html.

Coan, Blair. *The Red Web*. Boston: Western Islands, 1969.

Collins, Max Allan. "Ian Fleming." In Robin W. Winks, ed., *Mystery and Suspense Writers*. New York: Charles Scribner's Sons, 1998.

Conrad, Joseph. *Under Western Eyes*. November 2001. http://jollyroger.com/library/UnderWesternEyesbyJosephConradebook.html.

Cooper, James Fenimore. *The Spy: A Tale of the Neutral Ground*. Harmondsworth: Penguin Books, 1997.

Cowley, Jason. "Under Western Eyes." *New Statesman*, March 1998 [online]. http://www.jasoncowley.net/reviews/R19980320_NS.html

Crosby, Enoch. In H. L. Barnum, *The Spy Unmasked: or, Memoirs of Enoch Crosby, alias Harvey Birch, the Hero of James Fenimore Cooper's The Spy*. New York: Harbor Hill Books, 1975.

Deighton, Len. *The Ipcress File*. St. Albans: Triad/Panther Books, 1968.

Dekker, George. *James Fenimore Cooper: The Novelist*. London: Routledge & Kegan Paul, 1967.

Denning, Michael. *Cover Stories: Narrative and Ideology in the British Spy Thriller*. London: Routledge & Kegan Paul, 1987.

Diemert, Brian. "Graham Greene." In Robin W. Winks, ed., *Mystery and Suspense Writers*. New York: Charles Scribner's Sons, 1998.

Doyle, Arthur Conan. *The Hound of the Baskervilles: Another Adventure of Sherlock Holmes*. Oxford, England: Oxford University Press, 1994.

DuBois, William. "Graham Greene's Dark Magic." *The New York Times*, May 1943. http://www.nytimes.com/books/00/02/20/specials/greene.html#news.

Dulles, Allen. *Anthology of Great Spy Stories*. New York: Harper & Row, 1969.

Dupuy, Ernest R. and Trevor N. Dupuy. *The Encyclopedia of Military History*. New York: Harper & Row, 1986.

Eco, Umberto. *The Role of the Reader: Explorations in the Semiotics of Texts*. Bloomington: Indiana University Press, 1979.

Edgeworth, Maria. In George Dekker, *James Fenimore Cooper: The Novelist*. London: Routledge & Kegan Paul, 1967.

Epperson, A. Ralph. *The Unseen Hand*. Tucson, Arizona: Publius Press, 1985.

Follett, Ken. In Robin W. Winks, ed., *Mystery and Suspense Writers*. New York: Charles Scribner's Sons, 1998.

Ford, Franklin L. *Political Murder: From Tyrannicide to Terrorism*. Cambridge: Harvard University Press, 1985.

Franklin, Benjamin. In Donzella Cross Boyle, *Quest of a Hemisphere*. Boston: Western Islands, 1970.

Freemantle, Brian. *KGB: Inside the World's Largest Intelligence Network*. New York: Holt, Rinehart and Winston, 1982.

Fritz, Mark. "From Hot Conflict to Cold War." *The Boston Globe*, December 2001. http://www.boston.com/globe/nation/packages/secret_history/index9.shtml.

Goodman, Roy S. "Robert Ludlum." In Robin W. Winks, ed., *Mystery and Suspense Writers*. New York: Charles Scribner's Sons, 1998.

_____. "Graham Greene at 66." *The New York Times*, September 1971. http://www.nytimes.com/books/00/02/20/specials/greene.html#news.

_____. *Ways of Escape*. New York: Pocket Books, 1980.

Greaney, Michael. 2001. *Conrad, Language and Narrative*. Cambridge, England: Cambridge University Press.

Grella, George. In McCormick, Donald, and Katy Fletcher. *Spy Fiction: A Connoisseur's Guide*. New York: Facts on File, 1990.

Griffin, G. Edward. *World Without Cancer*. Thousand Oaks, California: American Media, 1974.

Hall, Stuart. "Notes on Deconstructing the Popular," in R. Samuel, ed., *People's History and Socialist Theory*. London: Routledge & Kegan Paul, 1981.

Hantke, Steffen. "God Save Us From Bourgeois Adventure" *Studies in the Novel* (28:2) 1996. http://library.northernlight.com/PC19970927440007896.html?cb=0&sc=0#doc.

Harper, Ralph. *The World of the Thriller.* Cleveland: Case Western Reserve University Press, 1969.

Hewitson, Mark. *Germany and the Causes of the First World War.* Oxford, England: Berg Publishers, 2004.

Hilfer, Tony. *The Crime Novel; A Deviant Genre.* Austin: University of Texas Press, 1990.

Himmelfarb, Gertrude. *Lord Acton: A Study in Conscience and Politics.* Chicago: University of Chicago Press, 1952.

Hitz, Frederick P. "Selected Issues Relating to CIA Activities in Honduras in the 1980s." *Report of Investigation.* Office of Inspector General, Central Intelligence Agency, Washington. August 27, 1997.

Hofstadter, Richard. In Steffen Hantke, "God Save Us From Bourgeois Adventure" *Studies in the Novel* (28:2)1996. http://library.northernlight.com/PC19970927440007896.html?cb=0&sc=0#doc.

Isaacson, Walter and Evan Thomas. *The Wise Men: Six Friends and the World They Made.* New York: Touchstone, 1986.

Jaeger, Karl. "Final Summary of Executions carried out in the operating area of EK [Einsatzkommando] 3 up to December 1, 1941." December 1, 1941. http://www.jewishvirtuallibrary.org/jsource/Holocaust/jaegerreport.html

Janik, Del Ivan. "No End of History: Evidence from the Contemporary English Novel." *Twentieth Century Literature* (41: 2), 1995.

Judd, Dennis. *Empire: The British Imperial Experience from 1765 to the Present.* New York: Basic Books, 1996.

Karl, Frederick R. "Introduction." In Joseph Conrad, *The Secret Agent.* New York: Penguin Books, 1983.

Kelly, R. Gordon. *Mystery Fiction and Modern Life.* Jackson: University Press of Mississippi, 1998.

Kelly, William P. *Plotting America's Past: Fenimore Cooper and the Leatherstocking Tales.* Carbondale: Southern Illinois University Press, 1983.

Knightly, Phillip. *The Second Oldest Profession.* New York: W.W. Norton & Company, 1987.

Kuan-chung, Lo. In Donald McCormick, *Who's Who in Spy Fiction*. New York: Taplinger, 1977.

Landrum, Larry N. *American Mystery and Detective Novels: A Reference Guide*. Westport CT: Greenwood Press, 1999.

Le Carré, John. *The Spy Who Came in from the Cold*. New York: Dell, 1965.

_____. "Le Carré on the Most Immoral Premise of All." *The New York Times*, July 1993. http://partners.nytimes.com/books/99/03/21/specials/lecarre-moral.html.

_____. "My New Friends in the New Russia: In Search of A Few Good Crooks, Cops and Former Agents." *The New York Times*, February 1995 http://www.nytimes.com/books/99/03/21/specials/lecarre-newrussia.html.

Lester, Juliuis. In Donald McCormick and Katy Fletcher. *Spy Fiction: A Connoisseur's Guide*. New York: Facts On File, 1990.

Lewis, Peter. "Eric Ambler." In Robin W. Winks, ed., *Mystery and Suspense Writers*. New York: Charles Scribner's Sons, 1998.

Liukkonen, Petri. "John Buchan." *Books and Writers*, May 2001. http://www.kirjasto.sci.fi/buchan.htm.

_____. "Ian (Lancaster) Fleming (1908-1964)." *Books and Writers*, April 2002. http://www.kirjasto.sci.fi/fleming.htm.

Lo, Kuan-chung. *Three Kingdoms: A Historical Novel*. Translated from the Chinese with afterword and notes by Moss Roberts. Berkeley: University of California Press, 1991.

Long, Andrew. "The Secret Policeman's Couch: Informing, Confession, and Interpellation in Conrad's under Western Eyes." *Studies in the Novel* 35 (4: 490) 2003.

Malmgren, Carl D. "Anatomy of Murder: Mystery, Detective, and Crime Fiction." *Journal of Popular Culture* (30:4) 1997. http://library.northernlight.com/SL19980512010144178.html?cb=0&sc=0#doc

Matin, A. Michael. "The Hun Is at the Gate: Historicizing Kipling's Militaristic Rhetoric, from the Imperial Periphery to the National Center." *Studies in the Novel* 31 (4: 432) 1999.

Maugham, W. Somerset. *Ashenden or the British Agent*. New York: Avon, 1951.

_____. In *W. (William) Somerset Maugham, British agent in World War I, (1874-1965)*. May 2001. http://www.angelfire.com/dc/1spy/Maugham.html.

McCormick, Donald. *Who's Who in Spy Fiction*. New York: Taplinger, 1977.

McCormick, Donald, and Katy Fletcher. *Spy Fiction: A Connoisseur's Guide*. New York: Facts on File, 1990.

MacDonnell, Francis. *Insidious Foes: The Axis Fifth Column and the American Home Front*. Cary, NC: Oxford University Press, Incorporated, 1995.

McHale, Brian. *Postmodernist Fiction*. London: Routledge, 1996.

McTiernan, Dave. "The Novel as Neutral Ground: Genre and Ideology in Cooper's *The Spy*." *Studies in American Fiction*. Spring 1997. http://library.northernlight.com/PC19970927600018576.html?cb=0&sc=0#doc

Melley, Timothy. *Empire of Conspiracy: The Culture of Paranoia in Postwar America*. Ithaca, NY: Cornell University Press, 2000.

Merry, Bruce. *Anatomy of the Spy Thriller*. Dublin: Gill and McMillan, 1977.

O'Brien, George. "John Buchan." In Robin W. Winks, ed., *Mystery and Suspense Writers*. New York: Charles Scribner's Sons, 1998.

Oglesby, Carl. *The Yankee and the Cowboy War*. Kansas City: Sheed Andrews and McMeel, 1976.

Olcott, Anthony. In Donald McCormick and Katy Fletcher. *Spy Fiction: A Connoisseur's Guide*. New York: Facts On File, 1990.

Oppenheim, E. Phillips. In Donald McCormick, *Who's Who in Spy Fiction*. New York: Taplinger, 1977.

_____. In David Stafford, *The Silent Game: The Real World of Imaginary Spies*. Athens: University of Georgia Press, 1991.

Palmer, Jerry. *Thrillers*. New York: St. Martin's Press, 1979.

Prange, Gorden L. *Target Tokyo: The Story of the Sorge Spy Ring*. New York: McGraw-Hill, 1984.

Quigley, Carroll. *Tragedy and Hope*. London: The McMillan Company, 1966.

Richards, Jeffrey H. *Theater Enough: American Culture and the Metaphor of the World Stage, 1607-1789*. Durham, NC: Duke University Press, 1991.

Ringe, Donald. *James Fenimore Cooper*. Boston: Twayne, 1988.

Roosevelt, Franklin D. In David Perloff, "Motives Behind the Betrayal." *The New American*, July 2001. http://www.thenewamerican.com/tna/2001/06-04-2001/vol7no12_motives.htm

Rosenberg, Bruce. *The Neutral Ground: The Andre Affair and the Background of Cooper's "The Spy."* Westport: Greenwood Press, 1994.

Ryan, Alan A. *Quiet Neighbors: Prosecuting Nazi War Criminals in America*. New York: Harcourt Brace Jovanovich Publishers, 1984.

Sandoe, James. "Dagger of the Mind." In Howard Haycraft, ed., *The Art of the Mystery Story*. New York: Simon & Schuster, 1946.

Schmitz, John. *Business Week*. (October 14, 1972), p.80.

Semmel, Bernard. *Imperialism and Social Reform: English Social-Imperial Thought, 1895-1914*. London: George Allen & Unwin, 1960.

Sharrock, Roger. *Saints, Sinners, and Comedians: The Novels of Graham Greene*. Notre Dame, Indiana: University of Notre Dame Press, 1984.

Showalter, Craig. "Somerset Maugham: World Traveler, Famed Story-teller." *The Caxtonian*, September 1997. www.caxtonclub.org/reading/smaugham.html.

Stafford. David. *The Silent Game: The Real World of Imaginary Spies*. Toronto: Lester and Orphen Dennys, 1998.

Standish, Robert. *The Prince of Storytellers: The Life of E. Phillips Oppenheim*. London: Peter Davies, 1957.

Sutton, Anthony C. *Wall Street and the Rise of Hitler*. California: 76 Press, 1976.

Symons, Julian. *Bloody Murder*. Harmondsworth: Penguin, 1974.

Thompson, Jon. *Fiction, Crime and Empire: Clues to Modernity and Postmodernism*. Urbana: University of Illinois Press, 1993.

Tibbetts, John C. "G.K. Chesterton." In Robin W. Winks, ed., *Mystery and Suspense Writers*. New York: Charles Scribner's Sons, 1998.

Toland, John. *Adolf Hitler*. New York: Doubleday & Company, 1976.

Tzu, Sun. *The Art of War*. Project Gutenberg Etext, 1910. http://all.net/books/tzu/tzu.html.

Walker, Cynthia W. "Spy Programs." *Museum of Broadcast Communications.* December 2006. http://www.museum.tv/archives/etv/S/htmlS/spy-programs/spyprograms.htm

Waples, Dorothy. *The Whig Myth of James Fenimore Cooper.* New Haven: Yale University Press, 1938.

Wark, Wesley K. "The Spy Thriller." In Robin W. Winks, ed., *Mystery and Suspense Writers.* New York: Charles Scribner's Sons, 1998.

Wier, David. 1997. *Anarchy and Culture: The Aesthetic Politics of Modernism.* Amherst, MA: University of Massachusetts Press.

Winks, Robin W. *Colloquium on Crime: Eleven Renowned Mystery Writers Discuss Their Work.* New York: Scribner's, 1986.

_____. "John Buchan: Stalking the Wilder Game." In *The Four Adventures of Richard Hannay.* Boston: Godine, 1988.

_____. "Introduction." In Robin W. Winks, ed., *Mystery and Suspense Writers.* New York: Charles Scribner's Sons, 1998.

Wolfe, Peter. *Graham Greene: The Entertainer.* Carbondale: Southern Illinois University Press, 1972.

Woods, Katherine. "Graham Greene's Stirring Tale of Beleaguered Souls." *The New York Times,* October 1939. http://www.nytimes.com/books/00/02/20/specials/greene.html#news.

Woodward, Bob. "CIA Told to Do 'Whatever Necessary' to Kill Bin Laden." *The Washington Post,* October 21, 2001. http://www.washingtonpost.com/ac2/wp-dyn/A27452-2001Oct20?language=printer

Yela, Max. 2001. *James Fenimore Cooper: Traditions and Interpretations.* Milwaukee: University of Wisconsin, Golda Meir Library, 2001. http://www.uwm.edu/Library/special/exhibits/clastext/clspg134.htm.

INDEX